Around the World
ON A SMALL MOTORCYCLE

J. Peter "The Bear" Thoeming

"I travel because I'd rather look back at my life, saying 'I can't believe I did that' instead of 'if only I had'."

FLORINE BOS

Copyright © 2023 J. Peter Thoeming

This work is copyright. Apart from any fair dealing for the purposes of private study, research, criticism or review, as permitted by the Copyright Act 1968, no part of this book may be reproduced, stored in a retrieval system or transmitted in any form or by any means, electronic, mechanical, photocopying, recording or otherwise, without the prior written permission of the publisher.

J Peter Thoeming – Around the world on a small motorcycle

ISBN: 978-0-6456123-1-8 (paperback)

 A catalogue record for this book is available from the National Library of Australia

Cover and internal design: Ronald Proft

Delphian Books
Unit 1, 29 Mile End Road, Rouse Hill, NSW 2155
delphianbooks.com.au

This book is dedicated to my daughters Alix and Louise. May I some time make them as proud of me as I am of them.

Contents

Foreword	v
PART 1: Sydney to the Guinness Brewery	2
Have a drink...	3
To Adelaide	6
Desert days (and nights)	10
Singapore	16
Malaysia	19
Thailand	27
Nepal	35
India	41
Pakistan	53
Afghanistan	58
Iran	66
Turkey	69
Greece	75
Yugoslavia	78
Italy	80
Switzerland	82
Germany and beyond	84
England, Wales and Ireland	86
PART 2: Three Continent Diversion	89
France	90
Spain	100
Portugal	105

Morocco	109
Algeria	122
Tunisia	128
Italy	132
Yugoslavia	142
Greece Again	147
Turkey Again	153
The Eastern Bloc and back to England	164
PART 3: Home Through America	171
The North	172
The South	182
The North Again	187
The West	190
AFTERWORD: The Bear, an overview	205

Foreword

This is an edited and condensed re-issue of the book *Motorcycle Touring* from Osprey Publishing in 1982. Today, which is to say in 2023, around-the-world-motorcycle rides are not rare anymore. You can even join a tour group and do it all in one go, or in stages.

Things were a little different nearly half a century ago. For a start there was far less information available. In retrospect, that was a good thing; we might have done things differently if we'd known what awaited us, and not enjoyed ourselves as much. As it was, the ride could not have been much better. Mind you, it could have been a lot easier...

Those of you who have been following my various stories on the web or in print, based on the journey described in this book, please note that those stories have often been fleshed out more than their versions here. What the book does is tie them all together.

Many things have changed in the past fifty years. For one thing, I don't seem to be able to run as fast or as far as I used to. But as Father Time has taken away, he has also given – I don't want to run as far or as fast as I used to.

And the international scene has changed both for the better and the worse. Although I love the place, I don't think I would ride through Afghanistan these days, and not just because I'd find it harder to run. You can't outrun a bullet. Likewise, I suspect that Iran would be a tougher nut – although I would trust to the basic kindness of its people. I imagine Burma (as it was then) would still be a hard nut to crack, as well.

I think I would take a different route entirely, from Thailand to China via Laos, then to Kazakhstan, Russia (but not during the current Ukrainian war), Georgia, Armenia and into Turkey that way. I haven't been to many of those places, you see. New people, new roads, new sights... Jack Kerouac was right when he wrote that "The Road is life".

But let's meet the protagonists of this trip. The year is 1977, and the place is inner Sydney suburb Rozelle, where Charlie (or Dr Charles Carter) and I (just me) were doing something we were quite good at – namely drinking.

PART 1

Sydney to the Guinness Brewery

CHAPTER 1

Have a drink...

CHARLIE AND I were comfortable. With generous glasses of whiskey in our hands we were lying back in overstuffed armchairs in Charlie's living-room. It was very late, the party had been over for quite a while, and we were talking in the desultory way you do at such times. Both of us were at loose ends. Charlie had nearly finished his thesis for a PhD in plant genetics, disclosing the private life of an obscure little wild flower; I was heartily sick of working in an advertising agency. We were both in our very early thirties. The talk revolved around alternatives, our bikes, booze . . . and suddenly it all came together in my mind. Or maybe in Charlie's.

"Why don't we ride over to Ireland and visit the Guinness brewery?"

Clearly it was time to become less comfortable. Our touring experience at this stage was fairly limited. Charlie had covered some amazing distances on his old Honda XL250, true, but it had been rallying rather than touring. My long-distance runs had been to get somewhere: opening the old WLA Harley up and pointing it at Melbourne, or perhaps my mother's place in Ballina, hardly counts as touring.

> "*I feel no pain, dear mother, now
> But oh I am so dry.
> O take me to a brewery
> And leave me there to die.*"
> **TRADITIONAL**

Although there had been one memorable trip. . .

My friend Campbell owned an eleven-year-old BMW R60 and we were going to the Intervarsity Jazz Convention in Armidale in northern NSW on it. Seeing that we had a bit of extra time, we thought we'd have a look at Queensland on the way. The first few hundred miles went quite well despite persistent overheating on the part of the bike. On the north coast of New South Wales we had our first flat tyre: the tube was butyl, but we didn't know that and fixed it the way you would a rubber one. Naturally, the patch came off again: flat tyre No. 2. We bought a new tube, but could only get one that was slightly too small: that lasted a day. The next tube was the right size, but by now the tyre was so badly split inside that it chewed the new tube up. Eleven flat tyres, three new tubes and one new tyre in three days, not to mention the steamroller that nearly ran the bike over in Yeppoon, was the final score.

It wasn't all like that, of course. We had some marvelous times in the little pubs and enjoyed the scenery and the riding. We enjoyed the jazz, too, when we finally made it to Armidale – but not the ride home; the bike seemed to have lost an enormous amount of power. When Campbell stripped it down after our return it wasn't hard to see why. There were hardly any rings left: that overheating must have done a bit of damage. Not exactly the most brilliant background for a bike tour around the world. We had by this stage decided that we might as well go on around the world, coming home via America. After all, once the bikes were loaded up...

The choice of bikes wasn't difficult once we sat down and listed

On the road, and practising to ride off the road down along the sand on the coast.

our requirements. We wanted single cylinder bikes, for simplicity and lightness: a single is easier to look after, to tune and to repair on the road, and when you have to ship the bike, be it by air or sea, the lighter it is the cheaper it is. Trail bikes, dual-purpose on-off road machines, seemed indicated for ruggedness. Some of the roads in Asia, and not only in Asia, don't deserve the name and road bikes can be a little flimsy. In addition, trail bikes cope with mud and rivers much better.

The bikes would have to be Japanese. It's bad enough trying to buy spares for fairly common bikes, but just imagine trying to find a clutch cable for a Malaguti in Rawalpindi. Neither of us liked two-strokes so the choice was simple – Yamaha XT500s or Honda XL250s. These days the choice is much wider, but in 1977 the only other four-stroke trail bikes around were tiddlers. I wasn't about to attempt the Afghani desert on a 125cc machine, so we settled for XLs, partly because Charlie already had one. I had little trouble finding another in good condition and at a reasonable price. Our friendly bike shop stripped the bikes down and checked them over: both bikes were found to have worn camshafts, and these were replaced, unnecessarily, as it turned out. Apparently XL camshafts wear to a certain point and then wear no further.

We bought some plastic panniers that looked reasonably waterproof. Jim Traeger, a friend of mine, a rider from way back and a descendant of the man who built the Flying Doctor's pedal wireless sets, made up strong cage-style steel carriers for them. These would double as crash bars, and they also carried one-gallon containers, originally filled with reagents, donated by a friend who worked in a hospital. One was designated for spare fuel and one for water. Plastic enduro tanks replaced the tiny metal fuel tanks on the bikes and we fitted larger rear sprockets for easier cruising. Charlie was given some aluminium tank boxes as a farewell present from the Botany Department at Sydney University. These had holes cut out of their bases which fitted over the filler holes in the tanks and were secured by the petrol cap. It meant unpacking them every time we filled up with petrol, but with the lids of the boxes locked, the tanks were effectively locked also. Unfortunately the electrical system of the XL won't support better lights and air horns, so we had to make do with the inadequate originals.

Then came the hard decisions. What to take? We packed a large and comprehensive first-aid box containing antihistamines, antibiotics and pills against malaria and stomach bugs, antiseptics, burn creams and bandages. In my experience you rarely use this yourself, but it comes in handy for people you meet along the way. Spares for the bikes filled half a pannier; they included cables, bulbs, electrical bits and pieces, chains, liquid gasket and WD40. Our toolkits were augmented by a set of sockets and an impact driver.

We would take a tent and camp until Perth, then send the tent back and use hotels and hostels for the rest of the trip. That sort of accommodation is cheap and convenient – and relatively safe – in the developing world. We bought wet weather gear, yachting clothes in my case, because I wanted the stuff to be light. Charlie bought heavyweight working gear: he was right, of course. His gear lasted the whole trip; mine failed me badly. Completely, really.

CHAPTER 2

To Adelaide

THE BIKES WERE finished in time for our departure, but only just. It is truly amazing just what can turn up to delay you, but we were ready when the first guests for our farewell party arrived. The bikes were all packed and lined up outside the front door. I will draw a considerate curtain of silence over the activities of the Sydney University Motorcycle Club that night. When the time came for us to leave, I had had half an hour of sleep, Charlie had had none and the guard of honour to see us off had shrunk from 80 to one. The entire club, barring only one intrepid soul, was asleep, some in distressing positions on the lawn.

> *"Australia is an outdoor country. People only go inside to use the toilet. And that's only a recent development."*
> **BARRY HUMPHRIES**

So were we, not long after departure. Not on the lawn. Our route took us through the Royal National Park south of Sydney, and we took advantage of a shaded riverbank to catch a bit of shut-eye: we'd done all of 30km so far. The afternoon saw us a little further along our way, but the weather was already demonstrating some of the nastiness it would be handing out later on. By the time we had passed Wollongong, some 80km from Sydney, a cloudburst had caught us. Its relatives followed us for the rest of the day as we rolled south on Highway 1 at the 80km/h pace that the XLs found congenial. We discovered a river cave to sleep in that first night, with a pool in front, but we left some of our clothes under a drip from the stone ceiling. A lot to learn, yet.

Julie and Trevor, friends of Charlie's, sheltered us the next night and tried to teach us mahjong into the bargain. Then we sat out on the verandah, looking out over their little bit of the Ranges, and had a few quiet drinks. Trevor, who is a clever mechanic, brazed up some braces for the backs of our pannier racks the next day. His workshop was across the road from McConkey's pub – "The Killarney of the South" so we ducked over there for a Guinness with lunch. They were out of Guinness.

We played boy motocross racers on some of the mud roads along the coast, and Charlie's Trials Universals beat my Avon Roadrunners every time. Not being much of a dirt rider, I was mostly petrified. Back on the tar, we rolled down through the state forests that straddle the border ranges, still in the rain, of course. But it's so peaceful down there, ridge after ridge of forest rolling away to the horizon.

Lakes Entrance provided fresh scallops from the local Fishermen's Coop, and I fried them in butter in my old Army dixie for a memorable meal. Lunch the next day was marine again, the Yarram Hotel turning out a seafood platter for $3 that consisted of grilled fish, deep-fried battered scallops, oysters and prawns with an excellent salad. Australian pub lunches can be superb, although the prices have increased over the past forty or more years.

Gippsland's straight roads took us further south, to Wilson's Promontory. This is a national park and the Department of National Parks and Wildlife makes absolutely sure you don't forget it. There sometimes seemed to be more signs than plants in the otherwise lovely, rugged, stony park. We camped at Tidal River among the black dripping ti-trees and drank quantities of bourbon and milk. For medicinal purposes only.

Friends put us up in Melbourne, and we spent a great deal of time in the excellent Chinese and Greek restaurants that city has to offer. As a Sydneysider, I am obliged to add at this stage that Melbourne doesn't have a great deal else to offer ... we take our inter-capital rivalries seriously. There being a shortage of helmets, we got around by car.

"Err ... this car has a bullet hole in the door," noted Charlie. Gaby, the proud owner, nodded. Apparently she had been driving along out in the country one night when there was a bang. When she got home, she extracted a .303 bullet from the padding in her seat. My friend Leonie grinned, "Who said Australia isn't the frontier anymore, eh?" she asked.

The Geelong freeway took us out of town a couple of days later and no one shot at us. We followed the Great Ocean Road west along the coast, throwing the poor little XLs around as if they were desiccated Ducatis. This is a marvelous bike road with twists and turns along the cliffs and a reasonable surface, spoiled only by some loose gravel and tourists. Lunch was at Lorne, in a pub that reminded me of the Grand at Brighton, then we were ready for the dirt and gravel surface after Apollo Bay.

Down to our campsite at the Red Johanna, the gravel was deep enough to swallow a bike whole, but we survived to sit on the cliff top and watch the sea mist roll in and envelop the coast in gauze. The next day took us through equal parts of state forest and grazing land to Mt Gambier with its famous Blue Lake, which every year it seems to claim one or two skin-divers looking for its mysterious water supply. We had a very Australian dinner at Mac's Hotel, the local cockie's pub. Cockies are farmers, not cockatoos (although that seems to be where the name comes from), and you can have cow cockies, wheat cockies

It's true we were on our way to Dublin, but not the one in South Australia.

8

or sheep cockies. I imagine that in the back blocks you can even have marijuana cockies... They all eat and drink well, as we found out.

The Coorong, a seaside desert rather strangely full of waterways, kept us amused the next day as we tried out its numerous little sand tracks. We needed the rest by the time we found a campsite on the shores of Lake Albert; I wonder what makes my body think that hanging onto the handlebars really hard will stop the bike from falling over? It doesn't work, you know. We left the pelicans nodding sagely on the lake the next morning and made our way up past Bordertown to Tailem Bend. Our first sight of the Murray River gave us not only a view of the longest river system on the continent but also of the Murray Queen, one of the last paddle steamers plying it. Very majestic she looked, too.

The run into Adelaide was a bit grim on the new ridge top motorway, which was exposed to the scorching desert winds. We had lunch at Hahndorf, in the German Arms pub; there's a large expatriate German community down here and they haven't forgotten how to cook a decent schnitzel. The Adelaide Hills provided a last bit of riding amusement before we rolled into the South Australian capital, dry and tired. Once again we had friends to put us up and put up with us, and Adelaide provided its famous Arts Festival for our amusement.

CHAPTER 3

Desert days (and nights)

THEN THE ROAD TOOK us towards the Flinders Range, and we registered our best petrol consumption figures for the trip: 77mpg, thanks to a substantial tailwind. Not far out of Adelaide we thought the end of the trip had come rather early as we rolled into a little town called – Dublin! We camped that night in Germein Gorge in the Flinders and had to be very careful with our fire – everything was dry; even the creek had long since ceased to flow. Fortunately we were already carrying our own water.

At Pookara, we turned off Highway 1 to go down the gravel road to Streaky Bay. The campsite was rather uninspiring, although the bay itself looked good with its alternating light and dark sea floor. We did find some inspiration that night in the pub, watching a little blonde, who was dancing in the tightest gold lame pants I have ever seen. Nothing was open the next morning, and breakfast had to wait until we reached Smoky Bay, where the General Store provided some geriatric biscuits.

> "*This is a country where even the fluffiest of caterpillars can lay you out with a toxic nip...*"
>
> **BILL BRYSON,**
> IN A SUNBURNED COUNTRY

It's grim country down there, but the people are friendly; Ceduna was pleasant enough, more like a suburb of Sydney than a town on the edge of the Nullarbor Plain. There we met a bloke who was touring the country in a converted bus. As a runabout, he carried a Kawasaki 1000 in the back – complete with sidecar.

Outside Penong there was a forest of windmills all mounted on wheeled trolleys – another testament to the inhospitability of the land. It wasn't much farther to the "Nullarbor – treeless plain" sign, where we saw our first wombat of the trip. He was just trundling along minding his own business, and disappeared before I could get the camera out.

Nullarbor, by the way, is from the Latin and apparently just means "no trees". That's reasonably accurate, too. The road is mostly straight and not very interesting, unless you find flat ground with occasional small, dried-out bushes interesting. There are signs warning of camels crossing the road, but we didn't see any of the actual animals. Camels were imported into Australia to carry supplies out to work parties in the desert and have multiplied in the wild. These days, Australia is the largest camel-exporting country in the world, so I'm told. I cannot vouch for this. Other animals which might get in your way out there are kangaroos, wombats, emus and wedgetail eagles. There are also innumerable but reasonably polite venomous creatures. As far as I know we export none of these, which does seem a bit strange.

To make camp, we went half a mile or so off the road and found ourselves a little sheltered hollow. There was plenty of small timber for a fire, and the stars looked the way they only ever do in the desert: cold, fat and piercingly bright. There are twice as many out there as anywhere else.

When we finally reached the coast the next day, we found a slip

We camped on our way across Australia, enjoying the space and crystal-clear night skies.

road that someone had bulldozed down to the waters of the Great Australian Bight. We couldn't resist it and took the heavily overloaded bikes down there. A shelf of rock at sea level had once contained petrified tree trunks, but these had been eroded away leaving vertical pipes through the rock. They now acted like fountains, and whenever a wave came in under the shelf it produced water jets of different heights.

Going back up the road was a comedy. The surface consisted of broken limestone on a bed of sand, and it was steep. I took quite a bit of it on my rear wheel, with Charlie laughing himself silly at the faces I was making. Then we had a 200km ride before we could get a beer.

There were lots of bikes on the road and a lot of dead kangaroos next to it. People will insist on driving across here at night. The crows and enormous wedgetail eagles were gorging themselves. A stop at Newman's Rocks, one of the few waterholes along the road, refreshed us and the long, sweeping bends as the road drops down from the plateau made riding interesting again.

We arrived in Norseman, the first town since Ceduna 1000km to the east, in quite good spirits after spending three days out in the desert. The new tarred road really makes the crossing easy. Norseman boasts a good, traditional pub that serves passable pies as well as Swan Lager. Highway 1 took us down its narrow, potholed length back to Esperance, which is blessed with truly beautiful beaches of fine, white sand and clear water; it's also cursed with the most comprehensive collection of signs forbidding anything that might conceivably be fun. We spent the evening, thoroughly depressed, in one of the local dives called, would you believe, "Casa Tavern".

Before leaving Sydney, I had wangled an invitation to stay with the west coast correspondent of Two Wheels, the bike magazine I was writing for. I now rang this unfortunate to advise him of our imminent arrival and to ask him for some help with tyres and spares. I'd forgotten that it was Sunday morning, and got him out of bed. That wasn't to be the end of Ray's troubles with us.

The rest of the day was spent dodging road trains - trucks with two and three trailers – and squeezing past a huge, wheeled hay rake someone had managed to arrange immovably across the highway. When we made camp, we could just see the outline of the Stirling Ranges through the evening haze. In the morning a short detour took us up to the foot of Bluff Knoll, where the national parks people, with an unerring eye for the most objectionable siting, had built an enormous brick toilet block so that you could see it 20 or more kilometres away. Bless their furry little heads. The Stirlings are still lovely, their steep but soft slopes covered in evergreen forest.

We lunched at Albany in the London Hotel, feeling rather homesick. Our local in Balmain is also called the London. It was a good lunch, too, and reasonable value for money. You can tell Western Australia is a prosperous state – food is dear and the people are dour. Wealth doesn't seem to cheer people up at all.

We didn't put our tent up that night, but slept in a little hollow in the sand hills at William Bay, cozy on thick grass. We swam out to the rock bar across the bay, and there was a gorgeous sunset. After Walpole, we reached the forest of great karri and jarrah trees which covers much of southern Western Australia.

The cafe at Pemberton had an old Seeburg jukebox, stocked with records of the appropriate vintage, and we amused ourselves playing "Running Bear" and the like. After a day of riding through chocolate-box scenery, we camped near Busselton and were confronted by a rather scary array of enormous insects. I've no idea what they were, but they were huge and looked nasty. None of them bit us, I will admit.

We found Ray's house when we got to Perth, and the key was in the letterbox as promised. By the time he got home from a hard day at the scrambles track we had emptied his refrigerator of Swan Lager. We sang the Swan Lager Song in an attempt to mollify him.

'Swan Lager, Swan Lager, you killed my old man,
Swan Lager, Swan Lager, kill me if you can, ..."

The agents for Palanga Lines, with whom we were to sail to Singapore, were helpful and told us to bring the bikes down to the wharf on the morning we were due to depart. Formalities were minimal. In Sydney we had been told to get here a week early, so we now had that week on our hands. The time passed quickly enough, mainly bikini-watching on Perth beaches and sampling various batches of Swan Lager as quality assurance. We also located an old Singaporean pal of ours who was running his own restaurant and discussed Lee Kuan Yew, the Angels and the martial arts with him. Hoppy knows more than most about all three.

Ray and Kerry hosted a very small (the four of us) farewell party on the night before our departure. The number of empty beer cans this produced is now, I believe, a legend around the Two Wheels office. Somewhat hung over, we watched the bikes being slung aboard our transport, the MV *Kota Singapura*, and then tied them down ourselves. They were down in the hold with a shipment of live sheep. Once boarding started, we staggered up the gangplank and found ourselves some deckchairs. Then we broke open the flagon of wine which we had, with uncanny foresight, rescued from the previous night's debauchery. Just as well, for the bar didn't open for hours.

The bikes in Fremantle harbour in front of our transport to Singapore.

Cabins were quite comfortable, there were a lot of congenial people on board, and it didn't take long for the trip to take on the atmosphere of a cruise. I started a water polo competition, which was incredibly rough and lots of fun. To be able to tell the teams apart, we played beardies against cleanskins. Us beardies cleaned 'em up every time. Mind you, it was mainly because we tried to drown as many of the cleanskins as we could get our hands on.

I also met Annie, the attractive, petite lady of whom you will be hearing more later in the story. A shipboard romance! You see, it does happen.

On talent night, we presented a musical version of 'Waltzing Matilda' (for the cognoscenti, it was the Queensland version) a traditional Australian poem concerning a sheep thief. Australian legends are almost exclusively about thieves of one kind or another. Charlie rustled a real sheep from the mob in the hold. Its stage debut was rather spoilt by the fact that it relieved itself all over the dance floor. But we were all nervous...

The Lady in Red is Mrs-Bear-To-Be, with me and a mutual friend.

CHAPTER 4

Singapore

THE PAPER TIGER, Singapore's preoccupation with paperwork, sprang as soon as we berthed. It was a Sunday, and therefore not possible to arrange the multitude of documents necessary to get the bikes off the ship. The ship was going back out into the Roads as soon as the passengers had been offloaded, and would not return until Wednesday. Palanga's agent was unhelpful to the point of being rude, and we had to settle for a bus ride to town.

Most of our fellow passengers were on a Sea-Jet tour to Britain, which included the sheep ship, a hotel stopover in Singapore and then a cattle jet to London. The driver of the bus taking them – and us – to the hotel was an optimist and pulled the old "whoops, we just happen to have stopped outside the shop of my brother, why don't you just look in" routine. I spotted a little Chinese hotel across the road and we ducked off the bus, leaving my camera case behind. After checking in at the Tong Ah, I discovered my loss quickly enough – and nearly had a heart attack – but the case had been offloaded at the tour hotel and I had no trouble getting it back.

> "*The Merlion is a mythological beast created by the Singapore Tourist Board in 1971.*"
>
> ENGRAVED ON THE BASE OF THE MERLION STATUE

Before Annie flew out to London, we had a couple of marvelous days together. We shopped, sightsaw and, of course, dined. Down by the harbour we discovered the statue of the "Merlion", Singapore's heraldic beast. It bears a plaque reading "The Merlion is a mythological beast created by the Singapore Tourist Board in 1971." Don't laugh; at least they know the difference between mythological and mythical (and mystical), which is more than most people seem to.

With Annie gone, it was time to tame the Paper Tiger, so we went down to the insurance office for Third Party insurance, valid in

Singapore and Malaysia; to the Singapore AA for an import license and a circulation permit; to the shipping office for a delivery order, and to the wharf for . . . the bikes?

Oh, no! First the bikes had to be lifted out of the hold. They were covered in a stinking film of lanolin from the sheep with which they'd shared their home. Then the wharfage had to be calculated. A clerk measured the bikes over the extremities, and arrived at a figure of two cubic metres each. This was transmuted, by the magic of Singaporean arithmetic, into a weight of two tonnes each. Just wait, I thought, until Soichiro Honda hears about his new 2-tonne 250cc trail bikes.

Clutching a form given to us by the measurer, we then had to queue for a delivery list. A very thorough questionnaire with three copies, this form actually demands the time of day – in two places. Is this some way of measuring how fast you fill out forms? Is there, perhaps, a prize? "Most Improved this month goes to Charlie and The Bear, who have come up...." A very kind Indian fellow-sufferer helped us wade through this.

We paid the wharfage and got the bikes, which refused to start. After a lot of pushing, swearing and checking of spark, we located the trouble. The carburetors were blocked by muck no doubt settled out of the petrol by the vibration on board. Red faced and still puffing, we ran the gauntlet of Customs and police, who checked all the papers. The sergeant in charge, a large Sikh, had a brother in Sydney who was stationmaster at Coogee. There's no railway station at Coogee, but I was not about to tell the sarge that. Singapore traffic, here we come.

We took full advantage of the city's attractions over the next few days: eating in Coleman Street; watching Chinese opera in Sungei Road; eating in Arab Street; delicious *roti pratha* across the road from the Tong Ah for breakfast; drinking the superb fruit juices made from real fruit in front of your eyes. It's a bike city, but most of them are 50 and 70cc tiddlers. Suzuki was advertising the "power alternative", an 80cc stepthrough. We saw a well-preserved Norton and two Gold Wings as well as a number of ex-War Department BSAs with girder forks and large sidecar boxes dating from WW2. Even some of the

50s had sidecars and delivered everything up to lengths of angle iron.

Singapore is a clean city. It might be more accurate to say that it's quite compulsively spotless, except for the waterways. Fines for littering are astronomical. I could well imagine living there for a while, but only for a while. It's all a bit too heavily regimented and conformist for comfort. When the time came for us to leave, we rode out on Changi Road and back around the reservoir to the border post at Woodlands.

A few years earlier I had entered Singapore here, and had had to buy a permit to import a deadly weapon (and simultaneously one to export a deadly weapon) for the sword I'd bought as a souvenir in Kabul. No problem this time, but our entry to Malaysia was not so smooth.

CHAPTER 5

Malaysia

DR MAHATHIR ALSO SAID that Malays are lazy. Perhaps, perhaps. I think that Malays just like to choose their own methods and priorities. Leaving Singapore, out on the Causeway, was much easier than coming in. The gentleman processing us at the Malaysian border was in civvies, and we had a little argument. I maintained that a Carnet de Passage was necessary for Malaysia, and he disagreed. "Perhaps I'd better see a Customs officer," said I. He drew himself up to his full four feet ten inches, threw me a withering glare and replied, "I am a Customs officer!" What else could I do but accept his ruling? I was to regret that later.

> "*The reason for Malaysia's peace and prosperity is because the people believe in sharing.*"
>
> DR MAHATHIR MOHAMAD, PRIME MINISTER OF MALAYSIA

We rolled out into Johore Baharu and soon found the way to Tinggi. A good if slightly bumpy road took us up into the hills and the rubber and palm oil plantations. With rain threatening, we stopped for a moment to don wet-weather gear and saw a chilling tableau. Up the hill towards us, into a blind corner, came two trucks side by side having a drag on the narrow tar. I was very glad we weren't out on the road...

In the little hotel in Tinggi I renewed my acquaintance with the dipper that takes the place of the shower in most South-East Asian countries. You just ladle water over yourself out of a large cement trough. It's marvelously refreshing after a hot, sweaty day. A little farther up the coast we filled our tanks for the first time in Malaysia and discovered that a full tank cost about as much as a hotel room and three meals put together, which is to say bugger all. This proportion was to hold true in most places in South-East Asia; half your daily expenses go for petrol, leaving half for you.

We rode on up the east coast, jungle swamps alternating with hill

A fellow motorcyclist in Malaysia with his ever-faithful WW2 steed.

plantations. I cashed a traveller's cheque at Mersing in a bank guarded by a little bloke armed with an enormous shotgun. Bit dangerous being a bank robber here, you could get hurt. Lunch was consumed at the harbour, overlooking the colourful fishing fleet. All the boats had eyes painted on their bows to enable them to find their way through the shallows, and presumably the floating rubbish. People were only too happy to be photographed and I snapped some enormous grins.

The little village of Nenasi, where we had intended to stop for the night, didn't have a hotel, so we went on to the regional capital, Pekan. Dinner of excellent *kway teow*, boiled and fried noodles, rounded off the day and we retired under the gently rotating ceiling fan. We left the luggage in the room next morning and rode the unburdened bikes up the beach. It was great fun and pleasant to be out of the traffic.

The South China Sea looked so inviting in the heat that we stopped for a dip, but the tepid water made it less refreshing than it might have been. When we came out, our feet had suffered a sea change – not into something rich and fine, as Bill Shakespeare has it, but into something black and sticky. The beach was full of blobs of half-solidified oil, no doubt washed from the bilges of passing giant tankers.

There was a fresh coconut lying on the ground near the bikes, and after a struggle I managed to get it open with my clasp knife. We found the milk refreshing and the meat delicious. By the time we rode back to town, the sun was high and very sharp. Fortunately, we still had our shipboard tans and didn't burn. Despite my tan, I was feeling pale and fat alongside the slim, beautiful Malays.

The Sultan's museum provided quite a bit of amusement. All his possessions seemed to be kept there, from the stunning collection of Kris knives to his old toothbrushes. You could even admire his used underwear, lovingly labelled – and of course carefully washed. We also found that Malaysian TV wasn't very Malaysian. After the news, they showed The Osmonds, and that was followed by Combat – dubbed. It was fascinating to see Vic Morrow opening his mouth and fluent – if badly synchronised – Malay coming out.

A bit of bad luck (and bad riding on my part) rather marred the next day. Just out of Kuantan, I glanced down at the map on my tank box. Charlie braked at exactly that moment for a large pothole and I ran into the back of his bike. Never look at maps on the move... By the time we'd picked ourselves up, it was obvious we were in a bit of trouble. Charlie looked as though he'd just been subjected to the amorous attentions of a sandpaper python and my arm and shoulder hurt abominably. Charlie also had a deep cut over his hip.

The locals could not have been more helpful and transported us to hospital. There they sewed Charlie up and put my arm in a sling, dismissing my claims to a broken shoulder blade. Never self-diagnose; it annoys doctors. It surely did the Peace Corps American surgeon who saw me. I dragged myself off to bed feeling like death warmed over and still sure I had a broken shoulder blade. When you've broken as many bones as I have, you know the signs.

Charlie commandeered a truck from the nearest bike shop and went out to get our steeds. Everyone was marvelous, from the chap who drove us to the hospital to the people who looked after the bikes. They were fixed cheaply and well while we convalesced, mostly by Charlie. One night, we went to the local fleapit to see Romulus and Remus with – guess who – Steve Reeves. The film was looking its age, and seemed to be intercut with snippets of at least half a dozen other movies. Kuantan was a pleasant enough town, but it did become a little boring, and we filled in the time with eating and drinking – mostly steamed dumplings and fish, washed down with the local Guinness or Tiger beer.

The locals take Guinness advertising very seriously and drink the stuff for its alleged health-giving properties, and every night they collected in a small crowd that marveled at this outstandingly healthy pair of Australians with their table full of empty Guinness bottles.

Then Charlie had his stitches out, and we were off again. Significant parts of his anatomy were still swathed in bandages and I couldn't lift my left arm. I had to use my right hand to put the left on the handlebar. We must have looked a fine sight rolling up to

Charlie looking his best post-crash with the repaired bikes in Kuantan.

the first army checkpoint on the road to Raub. There had been an attack on a police station and the army obviously thought us likely suspects, because they searched the bikes from stem to stern. But we were carrying neither explosives nor Communist Party membership cards so we were allowed to proceed. Once out of range of all the hardware being waved around, I started breathing again. I hate guns, and I make a special effort for Armalites pointed by what looked like 10-year-olds. Oh. All right, 12-year-olds.

In Raub, we were invited to park our bikes in the kitchen of the hotel. Then we went out and had a magnificent Chinese dinner, peering out of the windows at the army and what I took to be militia, who were riding around on Yamaha 70s with fierce-looking shotguns slung over their shoulders. Charlie went out to the hospital in the morning to have his wounds dressed, and on the way out of town we were nearly run over by an armored car.

There was an even more obliging parking space for the bikes the next night, in Kampar: the hotel clerk's living-room. He had his own bike in there as well. Another visit to the movies rewarded us with The Buccaneer, a 1958 epic featuring Yul Brynner with hair. When we got back, the disco downstairs was going full blast. They were boogying to *Rudolf the Rednosed Reindeer* and *Auld Lang Syne*; it was neither Christmas nor New Year. Funny town, Kampar.

The road to Penang was a main highway, with ferocious traffic that ignored our poor little XLs completely. I kept expecting to have to choose between ramming an oncoming and overtaking bus in the grille or ploughing into a gaggle of schoolkids on pushbikes. Tough luck, kiddies....

Once off the ferry in Penang we checked into the New China Hotel, of which I had pleasant memories. I'd stayed there seven years before, on my way back to Australia from Europe by bicycle and public transport. I even got my old room back. Then it was back to the hospital and another X-ray. I wasn't going to put up with the agony for much longer.

"No wonder you are in pain," the Indian radiologist said in that wonderful Peter Sellers accent. "You have a crack as wide as my thumb in your left shoulder blade." So I was strapped up and grounded for a week, and Charlie chauffeured me about on the back of his bike. We filled in the time pleasantly with Magnolia ice-cream, coconut drinks and lashings of satay with peanut sauce. As well as getting our Thai visas, Charlie had a new rear wheel spacer made up for his bike. The old one had worn away to a slim circlet of metal. We would have more trouble with that later... should have got more spare ones.

There were some other bikers staying at the hotel, including a German bloke on a Honda 500/4 and a Dutch chap called Frank, who had ridden a Harley WLA with a sidecar to Nepal and stored it there while he and his lady friend looked at Malaysia. I amused myself scribbling puerile philosophy in my diary. It's amazing what your mind will turn to when you're not feeling on top of things.

What is it they say about all good things having to end? I loaded myself up with painkillers, gratis from the hospital, and we took to the road again. I must say, despite the slight misdiagnosis at Kuantan, that the Malaysian hospital system is absolutely first class – and free, except for a nominal registration charge. Just as well, really. Neither of us had travel insurance, or any insurance except when we were forced to take it out, in Afghanistan of all places. That was obviously highly irresponsible, but we were young.

On our way up to the border we passed Butterworth Air Force Base with only a slight pang of homesickness at the sight of the Australian flag flying over the gate. It's an Australian base, the only overseas one our forces have, and I guess it's designed to protect the Malaysians from ... err.... yeah, well, maybe Dr Mahathir. The road to the border was enjoyable, with a good surface and long curves through hills covered with rubber plantations and carefully concealed gun emplacements. It looked exactly the way it had all those years before when I came through in the opposite direction on my bicycle.

There was comedy at the border. The Customs man wanted our Carnets. We told him about the bloke at the Singapore border and he started tearing his hair out. Of course we needed them! What did those clowns think they were doing? We left him still distraught before he could think of impounding our bikes, which he could have done, and headed for the Thai border several miles farther along the road.

CHAPTER 6

Thailand

MORE COMEDY AT SADAO as we filled out hands full of forms that made the Singapore Paper Tiger seem like a tabby. This is the Paper Dragon. One form had eight carbons, all but the first two totally illegible. Each copy required a duty stamp, with the total charge being somewhere around 12 cents. Then several officials had to see, stamp and sign the forms. Most of these gentlemen were out to lunch, so we joined them. A tip for you - the coffee shop across the road from the Sadao border post gives an excellent exchange rate. Tell 'em The Bear sent you and go "ooga, booga". They'll know.

We managed to get away in the end and ride the few miles to Songkhla, the first large town in Thailand. After finding a cheap Chinese hotel we rode out to the beach for drinks and dinner, which was not the smartest thing either of us has ever done. We sat in deckchairs out on the sand and had drinks. Many drinks, I think. We were drinking Mekong, the well-known Thai whisky, which allegedly

> **"Good guys go to Heaven. Bad guys go to Pattaya."**
> **ROADSIDE SIGN**

gets its name from the river because it looks and tastes like it. It does have a little more alcohol than the river water; at least I think so because the scenery moved in a rhythmic kind of way. We may also have eaten something. Later, very much later, we tore ourselves away from the pretty little ladies who had been serving us - if truth be known, they closed up and left us - and rode back to our hotel. Very slowly, very carefully, very crookedly and cursing the inadequate lighting on the XLs. Don't ever drink a lot of Mekong; it's not particularly strong, but the hangovers are awful.

The banks were closed the next day - it may have been Sunday - but we did manage to change some money at a large hotel and get out of town. Had Yai, which is the railhead for Songkhla, was dusty and confusing and we were glad to get back to the highway, but not for long. We were now open to attack from the huge Isuzu trucks that infest Thai roads, and spent quite a bit of time on the dirt escaping from them.

Hangovers abating, we rode through country like a Chinese woodcut with giant, almost unbelievably steep limestone outcrops flanking the road. Entertainment at our lunch stop was a couple of local lads trying to teach us how to pronounce Phangnga. You try it! They were agog when we lit our pipes. The Governor of the province, it seemed, smoked a pipe, so no one else did – the neighbours might think they were getting above themselves. We had another beer in the Governor's honour and then the lights went out – just a power failure, not a sign of official disfavour. Well, I guess.

The next day we rode on to the "Holiday Paradise" of Phuket Island, where we got directions for Patong Beach, the alleged hippy hangout, and rode out along an atrocious dirt track for a few miles. Right at the end was Patong Beach; we knew it was that because there was an enormous neon sign saying "Patong Beach Hotel".

The road out to Patong Beach was a dirt track through the jungle then.

The hotel was inhabited by Germans on package tours, but we checked in at the rather more modest Palmgarten and invaded the bar pavilion to sample some more Mekong – some people never learn – and watch the first squalls of the monsoon bending the leaves of the palms. This is a somewhat melancholy occupation, but in a good way. A few days of it convinced us that we'd better move on or be rained in, so we said goodbye to Sai Jai, the Thai lady in charge, and her assistants.

Charlie had become rather friendly with one of these ladies and left her an esoteric Australian T-shirt. Both of us felt better for having had a rest and made an impressive 573km to Thap Sakae on our first day. On my bicycle tour, I had inadvertently spent a night in a brothel here, which had turned out to be a good hotel as well. I couldn't find it again, so we settled for another lovely old timber hotel, all the wood lovingly oiled and spotless.

By the time we got to Bangkok, I had something else besides my shoulder to worry about – sunstroke. How do you get sunstroke while wearing a crash helmet? By exposing the base of your neck to the sun in the space below your helmet, that's how. I had been wearing only a singlet on top and the vicious sun had cooked my spinal fluid. It sounds worse than it was, actually; I just felt deathly ill for a few days and couldn't keep any food down. One way to lose weight. After I recovered, Charlie picked up a case of Bangkok belly. Another way to lose weight.

The city itself was, and I imagine still is, slowly disintegrating. Roads and footpaths were crumbling, the *klongs* or canals were stinking cesspits and as for the power lines... the most elaborate cat's cradle pales in comparison. There was a bit of a thunderstorm when we arrived, and some of the power lines were being blown together by the wind and were fusing, spitting sparks across the road and writhing in the air as they melted. Most street corners have their tangle of old, discarded wires aloft, ends waving in the breeze. Who knows which ones are live?

We booked into the pleasantly third worldly Sri Hualamphong Hotel at the main railway station and our bikes once more found a home in the lobby, the desk clerk lovingly spreading newspapers under them. While I was getting over the sunstroke, I lay in bed and listened to the frequent rainstorms drumming on the tin roof of the factory next door. I also drank gallons of the fresh tea that comes with the room. Once recovered, I sat downstairs in the lobby restaurant drinking beer and making occasional forays out into the city. Strange as it may sound, Bangkok is a stimulating, fascinating place even though it is falling apart or perhaps because it is....

The only thing that really makes it possible to live in Bangkok is the fact that it's inhabited by Thais. No one else could possibly be so stubborn and yet so gentle and relaxed in the insane traffic. No one else would be cool enough to survive. My hat goes off to the lot of them.

Not being Thais, we were quite glad to be taking the road out and heading north to Chiang Mai. Within the first 30km we counted four buses that had dived into the rice paddies by the side of the road. One of the locals with whom we discussed Thai road safety – by pointing and shaking an open hand – indicated to us that that was life. Or not, of course. *Mai pen rai.*

After that, as we turned off to the ancient capital of Ayutthaya, traffic eased up a little. So did the rain. Ayutthaya is worth visiting for its more or less well-preserved temples and Buddhas, monuments to the lavish devoutness of Thailand's Buddhist rulers. But don't buy the soft drinks. Being located at a major tourist stop, the refreshment stand charges up to ten times the prices common elsewhere. See, you knew there was a reason you bought this book, right?

For some reason I developed a craving for a tomato sandwich on black bread during our ride on to Tak. Thai tomatoes are weedy, weevil-eaten woody midgets and Thai bread is dry, sweet and indescribably awful. So that was one impossible dream.

Our hotel in Tak was another of those marvelous all-timber buildings, the wood hand-polished and lacquered; probably a dreadful fire risk, but so lovely. We reached Chiang Mai the next day after dodging in and out of the clouds along the mountain road between Thoen and Li. Like most Thai roads this one was quite well surfaced and twisted enough to make for interesting riding. It was also lined with forests of dripping, ghostly mountain bamboo.

I'd love to know why they put direction signs so far past intersections in Thailand. Why not right at the crossroads? This way, you never know if you've taken the wrong turn until you're a hundred yards past the fork, where you have to turn around and try your chances on another track, and go through the same thing again. It's like a game. Hey ferang, you think you're so smart?

Our base in Chiang Mai was the Chumpon Guest House, a spotless building with a common room, a garage and constantly available iced water. They did our washing for us, too. We found ourselves a tailor in town and ordered polyester safari suits with long sleeves. You think this is weird? It is not. I have this theory that you get better treatment at borders when you dress up, so we were taking advantage of the cheap tailors. A couple of days passed pleasantly with visits to the working elephants, who unlike the ones in "elephant refuges" in Malaysia seemed pretty well off and content, the waterfalls and the endless "antique" shops that dot the town. I bought a Buddha's head which, I was assured, was a genuine antique. When I expressed concern about being allowed to take a genuine antique out of the country, the salesman assured me that it wasn't that kind of genuine. A reminder of a few years earlier when I was shopping in Chicken Street in Kabul and overheard a salesman insisting that "Of course it is a genuine antique! I made it myself!"

The night after we picked up our suits, we went on a spree. This mainly involved having dinner at the Chalet, a ritzy French restaurant. We felt we deserved it, and what's the good of new clothes if you can't show them off? Dinner was a huge success with pepper steak and steak Dijonnaise set off beautifully by a '73 Medoc. It cost a fortune, but we felt like kings when we walked out. This sort of thing is highly recommended on any bike trip. Get out there and live it up every now and then, and a tent in the rain will be all the more acceptable for it.

I sent my mother a buffalo leather cutout figure from a shadow puppet play. The Australian Customs opened it, I later discovered. I

No matter where you go, you'll always find a fascinated audience of kids.

wonder what they thought I was sending my saintly old mum from Thailand?

On the way back down to Bangkok we visited another ancient capital, Sukothai – Thailand is lousy with ancient capitals – which was pretty, with the ruins all laid out in a grassy park that rather reminded me of Khajuraho in India. At the entrance, a policeman showed a rather unhealthy interest in the contents of my camera case. I fought off his increasingly stern demands to let him dig through it and was greatly relieved when we got away.

At this stage, apart from my spark plug burning out and being replaced and a slight oil leak around the head gasket on Charlie's bike, we had had no mechanical problems. That wonderful state continued, too.

We rode on to Phitsanlok, a rather ordinary railway town made interesting by the total absence of tourists. Our white faces and beards attracted rather more than their usual interest as we wandered around after dark. The next morning I did what I had been dreading I'd do. I didn't take my passport and traveller's cheques out from under my pillow when we left, and didn't discover the fact until we'd been on the road an hour or more. Naturally we raced back as quickly as we could, and as we walked into the hotel, the desk clerk stood up and gravely handed the stuff back to me. He refused a tip. I really don't deserve the nice people I meet.

We took a different route this time, up over the mountains, and had beautiful scenery for the rest of the day. A lot of this country is forest, alternating with little corn fields so steep that the farmers use ropes to get their crops down. I wasn't to see anything like this again until Vietnam, many years later.

Traffic was light on Highway 21 towards Saraburi, and the road good. We rode through a thunderstorm that was so dense it felt just like riding through a vertical river. The sun came out immediately afterwards and we were dry in half an hour. The sunset, over limestone cliffs, was dramatic. We made Saraburi well after dark, and for once the hotel had separate single beds. This is unusual in South-East Asia – single rooms contain a double bed, double rooms contain two double beds. Hmmm.

The short ride to Bangkok was enlivened by all the tiny Villiers-engined three-wheeled delivery bikes on the road. They looked cute, and they are incredibly useful – not something you can say of many people, except maybe Thais. We got back to Bangkok on Buddha's birthday and checked into the Sri again. Since we had been invited to park in the lobby last time, we just jumped the kerb and roared in. I'll never forget the faces of the people in the restaurant as we suddenly burst into the quiet of the lobby like motorised samurai.

There was no way we could get permission to ride through Burma, and no alternative route, so the next day we repacked our belongings to take maximum advantage of the 20kg baggage allowance we had on the plane to Kathmandu, and took the bikes out to the airport early in the morning. Eight hours of frustration followed. First, we had to make pallets for the bikes; we were sent over the road for timber and nails, borrowed a hammer from Customs and set to. Then there was the problem of reducing the dimensions of the bikes as much as possible. Like the wharfage in Singapore, air freight charges went by the maximum dimensions. We took the front wheels off, lowered the bars, removed the panniers, let the tyres down and unscrewed the mirrors. At least the nominal weight of the XL250s was only one tonne each, not two.

Charlie did most of the work, being a more dab hand with the spanner than I, but I had a job to do, too. I had to rush over to the main airport buildings to arrange the paperwork, a replay of Sadao, but urgent and initially without much help. An urchin eventually found forms for me. To cap it all, we had to bribe a Customs officer to make sure the bikes got on the plane, the only time I have ever paid a bribe to Customs.

We were dog tired and seething with fury – an interesting combination – when we got out to the road to catch a bus back to the Sri. Eight hours in well over century heat, without much shade and with constant frustrations.

Then the Great 21 Bus Mystery hit us. A gentleman at the bus stop told us we wanted a 21. So we climbed on the first one along, to be told that it didn't go past the Sri. "You want a 21." We were puzzled. "Isn't this a 21?" – "Yes, but you want a 21." We were beginning to wonder if "twenty-one" wasn't perhaps the Thai word for, say, 93. The fourth 21 finally took us. Back at the Sri, we immersed ourselves in beer and refused to come out. I sat there looking at a pepper pot with a winged bomb trademark on it and had some nasty fantasies involving Don Muang Airport.

Out at the airport the next morning to catch our flight, I realised that I'd packed my ticket in the pannier, which was on the bike, which, in turn, was already in the hold of the plane we were about to board. Full marks to Thai International. They listened to my story without even cracking a grin and issued a duplicate ticket on the spot. Sorry about the winged bomb thoughts, folks.

The first scotch after take-off tasted like – well, like the first scotch after take-off. Nepal next, and Nepal as I remembered it was a nice place.

CHAPTER 7

Nepal

I ENJOY FLYING WITH THAI, not only for the free scotch and champagne but also for the friendly cabin crews. We had a relaxing trip and arrived at Tribhuvan Airport in Kathmandu in good shape, where I discovered that I had not only packed my ticket in the pannier but my passport photos as well. The pleasant Immigration man shrugged, waived the requirement of a photo for the Nepalese visa and let me through.

An amiable three-hour wrangle with Customs followed about the bikes. They finally accepted our Carnets, and we were free to pick up the machines. "Pick up" was right, too. Our carefully constructed pallets had disintegrated and the bikes were on their sides, Charlie's leaking acid from the battery. A friendly bystander brought us back a gallon of petrol from town and we wobbled off on near-empty tyres looking for a service station. We finally found air at a tyre shop. Service stations don't stock it in Nepal.

> "One day's exposure to mountains is better than a cartload of books."
> JOHN MUIR

Which reminds me, don't ever ask for air in Malaysia when you want air. "Air" in Malay means water. So the Malaysian air force is actually the navy. True! Would I lie to you?

Once in Kathmandu, we parked in Freak Street and looked for accommodation where the bikes could be parked off the road. A young Australian woman, a computer programmer turned trekking guide, recommended the Blue Angel. Being Marlene Dietrich fans, we checked in there. It was roomy and clean and had a carport where the bikes could be chained up.

Despite being one of the most unsanitary collections of buildings in the world, Kathmandu is a comfortable, relaxed town. It's fashionable to think that all places are spoilt in time, but Kathmandu seemed

AROUND THE WORLD ON A SMALL MOTORCYCLE

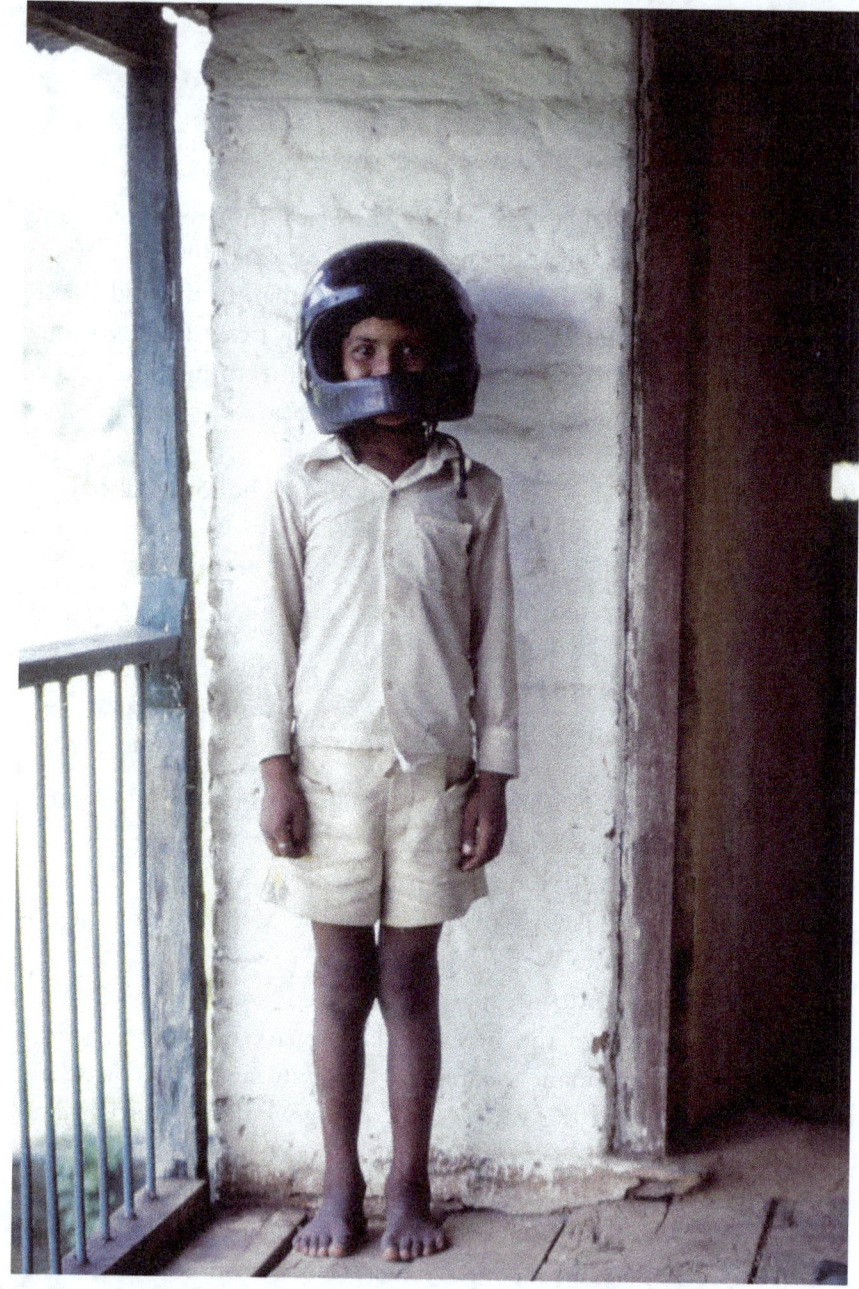

My landlady's son in Pokhara found my much-abused helmet the best toy ever.

better to me in 1978 than it had in 1970, when I'd last been there: fewer out-and-out derelict hippies, apparently less hard drug usage and a less frenetic street life, but all the little chai bars and restaurants were still playing *Dark Side of the Moon*.

I introduced Charlie to the peculiar Nepalese idea of European cuisine. We ate things like mashed potatoes with mushroom sauce, buffalo steak, lemon pancakes resembling citrus-flavoured inner tubes and cast-iron fruit pies. Not as bad as it sounds, actually. Gives your jaws a workout and it's bound to be healthy. Restaurants with names like Hungry Eye, New Glory, Krishna's and Chai 'n' Pie had survived. The New Eden reminded me of an exchange I'd listened to in there a few years back:

American voice No. 1, in front of counter: "Ah, how much are the cakes, man?"

American voice No. 2, behind counter: "Chocolate two rupees, banana two rupees, hash one rupee."

No. 1: "Ah . . . how come the hash cakes are cheaper than banana cakes, man?"

No. 2: "Because hash is cheaper than bananas."

One morning we got up very early to ride out to Nagarkot, a hill station near Kathmandu. We had hoped to get there before the mists rolled in and hid the Himalayas, but I got lost on the way, and all we saw was an enormous wall of cloud with Everest somewhere in the middle. Other day-trips went to Bodnath, the monkey temple; to the giant *stupa* at Swayambu; and to the river temples at Dashinkali.

We also "conquered" Pulchwoki, a 9050-foot hill behind town, on the bikes, travelling on a 14km dirt road up to the top. Wherever we went in the countryside, the sealed roads were covered in freshly harvested grain sheaves. The locals thresh in the simplest way possible – by letting the traffic run over it.

There was a bike shop near the Blue Angel. I peered in one day and was invited to inspect the premises. The tools consisted of a screwdriver and an extensive set of shifting spanners.

We secured visa extensions and took off for Pokhara, Nepal's

On the way up Pulchwoki, which you won't find in a list of Himalayan giants.

second city. The road was awful, more potholes than tar, until we passed the turn-off to Birganj and thence India. After that it improved dramatically and was serviceable even despite the occasional mud slide or washaway. It was built by the Chinese and follows the shoulders of the river valleys over three low passes until it gets to the plateau that holds Pokhara. Charlie went off trekking, walking up in the mountains along the paths that serve the local people as roads.

I checked in at a small, two-storey mud hotel and took it easy, bartering with the Tibetan pedlars, reading and writing. Tibetans are magnificent-looking people, like idealised Native Americans. They also have a great sense of humour. Or seem to, anyway. I couldn't understand their jokes, being totally ignorant of Tibetan, but their laughter was nice and inclusive and I never felt as if they were laughing at me. Could have been wrong about that, of course...

Being a little worried about drinking the water, I asked for a glass of boiled water at the hotel. I got it, too. A glass of boiling water – not quite what I'd intended, since I wanted to drink it. After that, I collected water from the roof during the frequent thunderstorms. The

I had lively conversations with the Tibetan pedlars without a language in common.

family running the hotel was very kind and kept offering me places in the buffalo stall for the bikes. I didn't think that was really safe; those buffs might have been good-tempered enough, but they were also enormous. The thought of one of them sitting on or leaning against a bike was a bit worrying.

Pokhara itself is a long, narrow town as yet little touched by modernisation. At one end it runs through large mango trees down to Lake Phewa, where the small hotels and shops catering for Europeans are. My shoulder was finally recovering, even though the torn muscles were still sore, and I just wandered around quietly. There was a lot to photograph, from the farmers arriving at the lakeshore in their dugout canoes to Machupuchare and the Annapurnas lifting their peaks high in the clear morning air. It's easier to see the mountains from Pokhara because the town is higher than Kathmandu, although you can't see Everest, which is too far away.

Charlie returned refreshed by his days in the mountains, and we took to the Siddhartha Highway, heading down to India. Nepalese friends had warned us that the road was "not very good": built by the Indian government, they shrugged. How right they were. The road is a nightmare of once-tarred dirt and gravel, but the scenery is superb – I think it is, anyway. As we came down through the deep river gorges, I wasn't often game enough to take my eyes off the road to admire it. Might want to go back there some time, like when I think it's time to shuffle off this mortal coil.

CHAPTER 8

India

THE NEPALESE CUSTOMS MAN glanced at the souvenirs we'd bought and asked, "Where's the hash?" with a grin and waved us through. We had donned our Thai safari suits and the Indians were duly impressed; nobody asked for driving licenses, insurance, vaccination cards or anything else except our passports – we were through in minutes. As we rode along shaded by great mango trees we diced with the traffic as far as Gorakhpur. Indian roads are alive with every kind of human, animal and motor-powered transport imaginable. The truck drivers, being Sikhs, are pretty well unbluffable and all else moves too slowly to be worth bluffing.

The Standard Hotel provided a welcome cool room. A gentleman I took to be the owner insisted on buying us breakfast next morning and involved us in a political discussion. It was his theory that Indians are so keen on politics because they can't afford any other kind of entertainment – politics is free. It also, he pointed out, mostly uses relatively few calories.

> *"Anywhere you go in the Universe, someone will always speak English."*
> MOTEL OWNER IN SATNA

We passed a funeral on the road that morning, the body wrapped in gold brocade from head to toe – a rather sad display of affluence among the drabness and obvious poverty. But each to his own. If you gotta go, go in gold brocade!

In Ghazipur we had intended to change some money, and consequently went looking for the bank. Despite repeated sets of directions, we couldn't find it. Eventually someone took us right to the door. We'd been past it several times, but there was no indication that it was a bank. It looked like an army barracks. It might just as well have been one, too; they would only accept US dollars, which we didn't have. Not even Sterling, and this in the land that remembers

One of the tamer carvings at Khajuraho. I recommend a visit if you're in the area.

the Raj so fondly! We revised the name of the town, in our minds at least, to Khazipur and left. *Khazi*, I understand from a British ex-soldier friend, is British Army slang for toilet.

On into the increasingly hot day to Varanasi, where one of the banks had a "late branch" in a hotel. We spotted a sign saying "cold beer" just outside, and Charlie was dispatched to investigate while I changed money. Not much luck for either of us. The bank clerk tried to give me rupees for $40 instead of the £40 I'd given him and turned quite nasty when I pointed out the "slight" discrepancy, and Charlie discovered that the beer shop hadn't had an ice delivery for a couple of days and all the beer was warm.

We retreated to the Hotel KMM, which had been recommended to us, and drank several gallons of tea and fresh lemon drink. It all went straight out again, mostly through the pores. On an evening stroll through the crowds of holy men and peddlers we acquired a friend, an eight-year-old boy who wanted to sell us some silk. He tagged along down to the river and introduced us to his father, who had just had his evening dip in the holy river. We sat watching the sunset reflecting in the river as the father told us some stories about Varanasi and the Hindu gods.

The next day was devoted to looking over such unique Varanasi attractions as the ghats on the riverbank, where corpses are burnt before being consigned to the sacred embrace of the river – a very quick look at that. Fighting off prospective guides took more time than anything else. We returned to our little friend's shop, in fact the family living-room and no doubt bedroom, and I bought some silk batik scarves for presents. They were beautiful, with motifs from Hindu mythology in rich colours. One hangs on my office wall to this day.

It seemed to us that the best way to deal with the heat was to get up early, do most of our riding in the cool of the morning and rest in the afternoon, and with that in mind we rose at 4am to discover that there was a blackout. We loaded the bikes by the light of our torches. The electricity came back on at about the same time as the sun came up. This little scheme did work quite well after that, though.

It was still cool when we stopped in Mirzapur for a cup of tea at the railway station and the road outside showed us the reason for the blackout. There must have been a storm the previous night, because a number of poles had come down and filled the streets with a tangle of wires. We ordered the "Vegetable Preparation", which is a selection of violently fluorescent pastes, presumably originally sourced from vegetables, in an aluminium TV dinner tray. It has little flavour beyond ha... ha... HOT!

We had a good road that day, still lined by mango trees inhabited by monkeys, and quite spectacular where it climbed the edge of the Deccan. Our host for the night was a retired lawyer-turned-spiritualist who now ran a hotel in Satna. He assured us that, wherever we went in the universe, we would always find people who spoke English. I guess a spiritualist ought to know.

A look at the erotic carvings on the temples at Khajuraho, which are incidentally very good and actually quite erotic, was followed by our hottest day to date. We pulled in to the courtyard of an Irrigation Department rest house and tried to find out from the chowkidar – the caretaker – if we could stay the night there and get something to eat. No luck. Our recently acquired few words of Hindi didn't seem to mean anything to him at all. What was the world coming to.

Lady Luck chose that moment to arrive in the shape of a short chap driving a locally made Fiat with a hang glider on top. He told us later that it was the only one in the country and he had brought it in under the pretext that it was a tent – substantial aircraft import duty would otherwise have been due on it. Tent duty, it seems, is more reasonable.

It appeared that we had not been able to communicate with the chowkidar because he only spoke the local dialect. Our newfound friend then reached into his car, where the thermometer (in the shade) read 52 degrees C, and produced two bottles of beer in dry ice, wrapped in a back copy of the Times of India, which he invited us to share with him on the verandah. The beer, that is. I could have kissed him. Sikhs, unlike Hindus, are allowed to drink – although they are not supposed to smoke. The bungalow, he explained, was not set up for meals. We thanked him for the beer and rode on to Jhansi. The heat, all the worse now we knew just how hot it was, was coming up off the road like laser fire.

Jhansi's Central Hotel was pretty basic, with those dreadful short charpoys – beds made of timber and rope and designed for Indian not Australian bodies – but there was quite a good curry to be had downstairs and we were entertained by a wedding across the road. A lot of the wedding seemed to involve firecrackers.

Next morning, road works gave us a bit of trouble on the way to Agra. A row of stones across the road can mean one of two things – either there used to be a broken-down truck there that's been repaired and moved, or there's a bridge out around the next corner. It's not always easy to tell if the road ends dramatically a few yards farther on. We were also getting sore backsides in the heat; XL seats are not comfortable at the very best of times and this was not one.

But the Taj Mahal took our minds off our worries. It is the only

The Taj Mahal is every bit as wonderful as it's said to be. Great back story, too.

building I have ever seen that lives up to the tourist hype, and we were fortunate enough to have a full moon to see it by. There were fireflies in the gardens, too, and it was almost unbearably romantic. Charlie and I would gladly have exchanged each other for female company. Sadly, this was not to be.

We found lots of mail waiting for us in Delhi, but the money that should have been sitting at the bank had allegedly not arrived. I checked every day, and one day in the lift at the bank, an aristocratic-looking Indian gent looked me up and down, said hello, ascertained that I was Australian and then asked: "What is your purpose in life?" I was still frantically trying to formulate a reply when we reached my floor and I beat a disorganised retreat.

The Tourist Camp in Old Delhi looked rather more comfortable than most of the cheap hotels, so we pitched our flysheet there over a large bit of carpet donated by the manager. Charlie did a bit of maintenance work on the bikes, among other things replacing the rubber seal on one of the fork legs of my bike. It had been weeping oil and proved to be rather badly scored.

Visas were a headache. The Afghanis weren't issuing any, having just had a revolution. The Iraqis wanted our passports for three months, to send to Baghdad for approval, so we decided to give them a miss. At least the Iranians only took two days. Outside the Iranian Embassy we met Paul, a fellow biker and a Sikh from Chandigarh who also intended to ride over to Europe. He invited us to come and stay with his family when we passed through Chandigarh, and we gratefully accepted.

We had a lot of trouble with our money transfers to Delhi and waited for over a week. It was partly the fault of our bank back in Australia, but the Indians certainly weren't overly organised. After we had covered Delhi's tourist attractions we whiled away the time in the US Information Service and British Council libraries which offered air conditioning and newspapers. We also bought some sheepskins and made them into seat covers for the bikes. Our money came eventually; Charlie found the advice for his while glancing idly through one of the file folders in the bank. Like they say, if you want something done...

Crossing the bridge out of town over the Yamuna River was like riding through a suburb of hell. It was a closed, boxy steel affair and hot, claustrophobic, slippery with dung, and predictably enough it stank. The roads up to the foothills of the Himalayas weren't much, either. We passed a totally flattened three-wheeler van lying in the ditch.

We were on our way up to Rishikesh, yet another holy town. Hardwar, at the entrance of the valley, looked interesting with its hundreds of little shops in booths lining the road, but Rishikesh itself was more like a Hindu Disneyland, complete with helicopter pads for the affluent gurus. Down by the river we met one who was still working his way up. "I have only one disciple so far," he said, "a Swiss man. But there will be more in time, do not fear."

The road over to the old British hill station of Shimla was better. Lined by pine trees, it was chiseled into the sides of the hills. Every now and then the fog lifted and opened out spectacular views of

Charlie's open-air workshop at the New Delhi campsite, working on my bike.

hillsides and forest. There were some river fords, too, crossed amid much white water, and very little traffic, a great relief after the crush down on the plains. For a while the road ran parallel to the Shimla railway, which looks like a big toy with its narrow gauge.

Our stay with Paul's family in Chandigarh was enjoyable too - they were non-orthodox Sikhs, very middle class and very kind. We had some more maintenance to do. Charlie's bike was still showing a slight oil leak at the head gasket and my shift drum stopper bolt had shorn through. A friend of Paul's got his father to make us a new one out of surgical steel, far better than the old with a small ball bearing, and Paul's brother JP arranged for me to go to the hospital and have a nasty boil on my arm lanced. You know, housekeeping.

By the time we left, the local boys had become rather dissatisfied with their bikes. The Yezdis they were riding, locally built Jawas, lagged rather noticeably behind the Hondas in sophistication. We left them trying to devise a way of improving the rear suspensions to XL standards. The Grand Trunk Road swallowed us, on our way to Jammu and Kashmir.

At a truck stop on the main road we finally managed to get a proper hot curry. Indians tend to be very solicitous of Europeans - they don't believe we can eat their curries. Should you attempt to order one you will usually be served a boiled egg on toast instead. In this case there was no option, they only had one pot. Charlie and I, being experienced curry consumers, amazed this lot by going back for second helpings.

Just before Jammu we found a back road that would cut a few miles off the run to Kashmir, and followed it up into the hills. We also found that Charlie's engine was covered in oil ... he'd done the tappets in Chandigarh and only finger-tightened some of the bolts. Then my clutch started to slip. We still managed to enjoy the little back road, surrounded by fantastic cliffs carved out of the soft soil by rapid erosion. Potentially a bit dangerous, though. I can well imagine entire sections of roadway disappearing downhill in a rainstorm.

Staying at the Green Hotel in Udampur seemed like a good idea at first, until we discovered that there was no water for showers or washing and the room next to ours was being used for a party by a crowd of very drunk Sikhs from a nearby army base. As I've mentioned, Sikhs are not allowed to smoke, but we discovered that they take maximum advantage of being allowed to drink... Charlie refused to pay more than half of the bill in the morning and read the riot act to the proprietor in a way I still admire today.

The road to Kashmir is rather like a badly tarred motocross track, and about as much fun, which is to say that we enjoyed it as long as there were no trucks trying to run us off the edge of the road. Sometimes there was a drop of hundreds of metres (I kid you not) straight down from the edge of the road to the river, and no safety barriers. Some of the mudslides across the road had been here so long they had been given names, on little concrete markers. I suppose it's easier than doing anything about them.... Just before we got to the 2.5km tunnel that leads into the Vale of Kashmir we passed a military convoy of well over a hundred trucks. The tunnel itself is a nightmare with very poor low-wattage lighting, no reflectors and icy drips from the ceiling. Remember we were on XLs, with their notoriously dim headlights.

Kashmir is a beautiful place and it's easy to see how it gave rise to the legend of Shangri-La, the paradise high in the Himalayas. Everything is green, there are majestic poplars lining the roads and the ground seems to ooze fertility. It has its problems, though, for the visitor. Kashmir is a holiday resort for thousands of people from India and is set up accordingly.

The touts trying to sell you souvenirs, a hotel room, a bed on a houseboat or leather clothing can become very trying. They nearly threw themselves under the wheels of the bikes, business cards clutched in their hands, when they saw us coming. Ignoring them, we stayed in the faded Victorian splendour of Houseboat Golden Rod, our every wish catered for. Well, nearly. The Mughal gardens and floating palaces are worth seeing and shopping is good. We had some leather vests made by Aruga The Robber (his shop sign) very

Aruga The Robber's shopfront. The bloke with glasses is the man himself.

cheaply, but alas not very well.

The road up is also the road down. We played chicken with another military convoy, buzzed through the heavily fortified town of Jammu – it's near the Pakistani border – and back out onto the plain. A South African bloke we met was travelling on a Dutch passport because South Africans weren't allowed to enter India. He had a two-day-old Indian Enfield 350 with which he'd covered 200km. In that distance he had broken the throttle and front brake cables as well as losing the battery cover and the bolt holding the exhaust in place. He didn't think that was bad, and anyway there were bike repair shops everywhere.

It would have been an understatement to say that we were hot, and we attempted to order a couple of bottles of beer that night to go with our dinner. The waiter waggled his head and indicated that this was in fact a "dry day". A number of Indian states have various kinds of prohibition, and we were unable to buy beer. In at least one state you have to register as an alcoholic to get a drink at all. "Strictly for medicinal purposes..."

I looked the waiter in the eye and said, very slowly and with minimal inflection, "I don't think you heard me. We would like *two bottles of beer*..." He folded and sent the eighty-year old "boy" out for the amber nectar. When he returned and placed the bottles on the warm marble tabletop, they were so cold that one exploded. He shrieked and ran and we made do with one bottle.

There was an enormous crowd around when we loaded the bikes up in the morning. In a country of crowds, where foreigners seem to draw them like honey does bees, you get used to them. This one was extraordinary though – commerce ceased all over town as everyone watched us. We had to deliberately tread on people's toes to get to the bikes. It was scary, even though there wasn't the slightest feeling of hostility.

A little later, the skies opened and the monsoon proper had begun. Within a few minutes the carriageway was 15 to 20 cm deep in water – muddy water. This meant that not only was the rain obscuring our sight of the way ahead, but the potholes were invisible too.

In the Amritsar Youth Hostel we met Jajime, a Japanese chap who'd ridden a Yamaha DT125 from Calcutta to Kayseri in Turkey and was now on his way back. He thought the DT was "perhaps a little slow for the long roads". While in Amritsar we duly admired the Golden Temple, spiritual home of the Sikhs. One distinguished-looking gentleman took my hand at the entrance to the temple, squeezed it and pushed a Sikh bangle over the hand onto my wrist. He charged me a rupee for it, which I thought was reasonable seeing it's stainless steel and can be used as a crown seal bottle opener. It is still on my wrist after 40 years and has opened innumerable bottles of beer.

We then headed for the Pakistani border. On the way, I swerved to miss an elderly gent on a bicycle and fell over. My chain came off and the inevitable crowd gathered while we replaced it. Charlie finally lost his temper and pushed a young bloke who obstinately kept getting in his way. Not very hard, but I was concerned how the crowd would take it. They fell about laughing.

We crossed the border at the same time as an unbelievably well equipped party of British Army mountaineers. They were Royal Engineers returning after a few months in the Himalayas on full pay. Could it be that there's something to be said for the army after all? Indian Customs and immigration processed us politely, though not promptly – they weren't together enough for that – while they bossed a motley crowd of hippies around rather brusquely. The Border Safari Suit Ploy works again!

CHAPTER 9

Pakistan

THERE WAS A DIRE SHORTAGE of pens at the Pakistani border post. All the guards kept borrowing each other's, which tended to slow things down a bit. I finally donated one of my treasured Nikkos to the bloke who was processing us and we were through in seconds. My second case of bribery, but a cheap one.

On the dusty road to Lahore we noticed the difference in road manners compared to India. Everybody was much more together and aggressive, which made the traffic rather more predictable if also potentially lethal.

The Australian AA guidebook gave us a bum steer to the location of the Pakistan AA guest house. They didn't even have the right street. As a result it took us hours to find it, and we were sorry when we did. It wasn't so much the decaying cars outside or yet the mould on the walls and the broken windows, it was the constant drip of every tap in the place that bothered me. We took it anyway, because it was also dirt cheap. Then we set off to find some food and cheer ourselves up.

> "*Expect the best, prepare for the worst.*"
>
> MUHAMMAD ALI JINNAH, THE FATHER OF PAKISTAN

The Capri Grill in the Mall provided excellent chicken livers and terrible chips. The Mall itself was well worth a look, with the enormous Zam Zam gun referred to in Kipling's Kim at one end and the slums discreetly tucked away at the other. But even so Lahore is quite a leafy and attractive place; its Red Mosque is allegedly the largest in the world. You can go and look at it, too, which makes a change from all the closed houses of worship some religions go in for, which seems a bit self-defeating to me.

The road to Rawalpindi looked like a left-over set from a disaster movie. It was difficult to decide whether it was being repaired or had

Yes, Pakistan does have pizza parlours. Well, kind of. No toppings, for one thing.

simply been abandoned. We weren't clear of the monsoon yet, either, so we rode in a downpour most of the day. My speedometer cable broke, too, but at least the weather was warm.

All the cheap hotels in 'Pindi were mysteriously full, and we wondered for a while if we had a disease that the hoteliers could smell and we couldn't. A kindly gentleman finally explained that the government doesn't allow cheap hotels to rent rooms to Europeans; whiteys have to go to the expensive ones. His cousin, however, happened to own the Alia Hotel, which was not too expensive, clean and comfortable and had room for the bikes in the lobby as well as an en suite bathroom and toilet. This turned out to be just as well...

At dinner across the road, while trying to choose between the usual gristly mutton, athletic chicken and slimy marrow curries, we drank some bottled water with ice in. The ice, as we should have known, was a mistake. Our reward was a painful case of the local equivalent of Delhi Belly, the Rawalpindi Runs. Both of us featured delicate pale green faces, dizziness, diarrhea and vomiting – for three days. Hence the convenience of the ensuite conveniences. It had actually never

Pakistani trucks are literally works of art. Driving involves a lot of faith in fate.

occurred to me that, when someone says "I turned green," they might be speaking literally. As Eccles says, you learn something every day.

Somehow amongst all that we still managed to get out to the Afghani Embassy in nearby Islamabad, Pakistan's Canberra, to apply for visas. Here they explained that the visa section was at Nigeria House, across the town. Who said there's no cooperation among Third World nations? On the way we had to stop several times and remove our wet weather gear. Well, the pants anyway. We reached Nigeria House and, yes, we could get visas, for seven days. Come back tomorrow to collect them. It beats me why you always have to wait for visas, when all they are is a stamp in your passport. It's just attempted intimidation. But then with my gurgling stomach I wasn't exactly in the best possible mood.

We picked up the visas when we had recovered a little and headed for the border. Within the first couple of miles we were both stung by monster wasps, the side of my face swelling up until I looked like a Dick Tracy character. Bubbleface, perhaps. Fortunately I got my helmet off before the swelling really got going; otherwise I might have

Public transport in northern Pakistan mainly involves finding space for yourself.

been trapped in it. Apart from that the road north was pretty dull, although enlivened by the marvelously colourful trucks and buses; the paintings on some of them would be the envy of any Californian customiser.

Peshawar, especially the military cantonment, was pretty and green.

At the gate to the Khyber road, there's a sign that warns you that once past the gate you're on your own – the government takes no responsibility for you. During the hours of darkness nobody is allowed in at all. It's not terribly hard to see why they're so careful. All the male locals carry bandoliers and well-used .303 rifles, and they look tough. These are the Pathans of song and story, and they'd make it to president in any patch club I've ever seen – without even riding a bike.

The road through the pass is surprisingly good, although infested by cars and pick-up trucks all carrying more passengers than you'd think possible. They take the boot lids off the cars and passengers sit there and on the roof rack while the family of the driver travels inside. Everybody grins and waves, which takes the edge off the universal toughness a bit.

Up through the pass the cliffs are lined with the badges of British and Indian regiments that fought here. There are a lot of badges. Villages feature high walls and watchtowers. The border town is called Tor Khan and consists of a number of mud huts collectively defying gravity. One of the more ragged-looking edifices is the Tourist Hotel, which, while it may not have running water, does have cold beer as well as a very entertaining proprietor.

Another form of entertainment in Tor Khan is gun shopping. Every shop – even the soft drink bar – has its display of small arms. These are all locally made, despite the lovingly forged "Smith & Wesson" and "Birmingham Small Arms" badges featured on the guns. Beautiful workmanship, though. I guess it would have to be. A warranty problem could lead to some pretty serious results up here.

CHAPTER 10

Afghanistan

"When you're wounded and left on Afghanistan's plains,
And the women come out to cut up what remains,
Jest roll to your rifle and blow out your brains
And go to your gawd like a soldier."
RUDYARD KIPLING

THERE ARE ONLY TWO categories of the compulsory Afghani vehicle insurance – vehicles with more than eight seats or fewer. This meant that we had to pay the same rate as a minibus. But we got our own back on the Customs bloke. He only knew three words of English, "I must look ...", and he kept saying them as he stood in front of our carefully packed and locked machines. We said "OK, look," and ignored the fact that he wanted us to unlock everything. He was actually rather nice, and finally took readings from our odometers to cover his embarrassment and left, muttering "I must look..." I presume he was headed for his English teacher.

If you don't understand our glee at beating the Customs for once, you've never been through a bad border. Our joy didn't last long, of course. Karma struck. Within a few minutes, still in the pass, I had a flat tyre, our first on the trip. There was a largish tack in the front tyre, which we fixed as quickly as possible, because it was hot again and there was no shade.

We were well and truly out of the monsoon now and would see no more rain until the Black Sea in Turkey. Jalalabad, the first stop north of the Khyber, was a friendly if slightly rough town, and we stopped for one of the local hamburgers and 20 or so bottles of Coke. The old bloke deep-frying the meat asked us if we wanted salad. Is the Pope Catholic? Of course we wanted salad. He gave us each a great handful of roughly chopped onion.

Yours truly in the Kabul Gorge, rather tentatively admiring the roadside cliffs.

Then on to the middle of town where there was an intersection vaguely like a roundabout, featuring a lot of those fiddly little cement islands, and meant to channel traffic in the right directions. We were still getting used to riding on the right – it changes at the Afghani/Pakistani border – and wove our way around in different but about equally wrong paths. The policeman on point duty watched, first with an open mouth and then with a huge grin.

We swam in the icy Kabul River just below Kabul Gorge, one of the most spectacular bits of road building around. The road just climbs up a vertical rock wall, with switchbacks and tunnels every few yards. At the top of the gorge an XL250 went past us, going the other way. Huh? Paul, the rider, was on his way home to Australia from Britain. He had made the mistake of riding at night in Iran. A broken arm had taught him not to do it again.

At a roadblock near Kabul, the army checked our papers. The officer in charge looked at our passports and said, "Aha, Australia. So you do not speak English?" We solemnly shook our heads and he waved us through.

Next came our introduction to the Great Game, of buying petrol that is. To understand how this works, you must know that the pumps only show quantity, not price. So you fill up and give the attendant some money. He stands there and smiles at you. You hold out your hand and demand change. He gives a little start – oh, sorry! – and gives you a little money. Then he stands there and smiles at you again. You repeat your act, he repeats his. This goes on until you either have all your change or give up in disgust. It's best to have the right money in the first place. You can actually work out the cost because petrol, we eventually discovered, costs the same all over the country.

There was no trouble finding a hotel in Kabul; we ended up in what looked as if it might once have been a substantial bank. Then it was out for dinner on Chicken Street, a thoroughfare full of shops selling genuine antiques. Once again, not that kind of genuine – although I once bought a sword here which was genuine if dilapidated and which got me into no end of trouble in Singapore. We ate delicious

One of the mighty Buddha statues at Bamian, now sadly destroyed.

minced-goat kebabs and drank delicious tea in one of the many filthy, comfortable chai khanas or tea houses, and took stock. Our visas weren't long enough for us to take a trip up to Bamian, but we both wanted to see it – in my case again. One-week visa extensions took four days to get, which wasn't really worth it, so we decided to simply overstay and pay the fine when we left.

A day was spent in the dusty and totally enchanting Kabul bazaar, watching absolutely medieval things like the water delivery – it comes in goatskins. Then it was off along the Mazar road, a well-surfaced and Russian-built tar highway to the USSR border. After about 100km, we turned off onto the 160km gravel track to Bamian. The track winds through the Koh-e-Baba mountains, with some breathtaking gorges and blasted, lonely plateaus on the way. I was a bit too keen and encountered a minibus as I was taking a corner on the wrong side of the road. Result, one dropped bike with twisted forks. We straightened them by the roadside, watched by a trio of goatherds, and not long afterwards I had another flat tyre. But, let me add, none of this spoilt the ride for us.

A young teacher invited us in for a cup of tea and we discussed politics without more than three words in common, except for proper names. He was in favour of the Communist revolution ("*kommunis* [thumbs up]") which had just taken place – the first of three which culminated in the Russian takeover two years later – but he was violently anti-Russian. I wonder what he's doing now... Our landlord in Kabul had warned us to make sure that everyone knew we weren't Russians. Otherwise – he mimicked cutting his throat – we would wake up dead. The teacher more or less confirmed this for us.

Bamian, which is nearly 3,000 metres high, was cool and quiet. We moved in at the Marco Polo Motel – the owner insisted that the man himself had stayed there but admitted he didn't know in which room – and went off to inspect the magnificent 50-metre-high statues of Buddha. They were carved out of the rock in the fourth century, when the monastery here had thousands of monks. Genghis Khan chopped their faces off some 800 years later. Genghis also destroyed the old city of Bamian, now an eerie collection of ruins on a hilltop called the City of Noise from the way the wind whistles through it. They remember the Great Khan well up here in Afghanistan, if none too kindly. His worst act, one of the guides told us, was not to kill practically everybody but to destroy the qanats, the underground irrigation water supply.

The Ayar Valley, around the new Bamian, is an oasis of fertility in the grim mountains, kept green by irrigation water brought many kilometres from the melting snows by a few remaining qanats and more modern techniques. Tourism has done its work, unfortunately; the children greet strangers with "Hello, *paise*". *Paise* is the local word for money.

We looked at the Red City on the way back. This is another ruined hilltop town, built of red mud and now melting down the cliffs in the infrequent rains. Then, on the road again, I did something very foolish.

Thinking I had been seen by the driver, I made to overtake a truck on the right. Just as I was level with it, the driver pulled over and inadvertently (I presume) ran me off the road. I went down a 10 metre, 45 degree embankment, weaving my way through huge boulders, into a field, where I stopped the bike and shook for a while.

Back in Kabul, we couldn't believe ourselves in the mirror. We were covered in a fine, grey dust and looked about 90 years old. A shower soon fixed that, but at a price. The Kabul water supply comes straight off the melting snows, and you step out of the shower blue with cold. Still, as everyone says, it's very refreshing.

The next day, we had cholera booster injections before departing. The clinic was in an unmarked flat in a dubious-looking concrete block on the fringe of town, which was a bit of a worry, but we had been warned and had brought our own, new needles. We donated them after the injections, which went over very well.

The Kandahar road is dull, but the surface is good. "It was built by the Americans," we were told. We had intended to stop in Ghazni, but the government hotel had no water and the alternatives were dirty and expensive, so we pushed on to Kelat. Along the way we saw an Afghan hound herding some sheep, the only time I've ever seen one of these beasts at work.

Further on a small boy thought he'd impress his friends by throwing a rock at me. Now I don't think this sort of thing is a good idea at all, so I turned around to go back and point out the error of his ways. He took off across the fields, running for all he was worth, and lost his cap, his satchel and the respect of his friends all at the same time.

After a night in the hotel-cum-police station at Kelat (we couldn't work out which it was, and it was probably both) as paying guests of the national police we made Kandahar without further incident. Except for the Attack of the Suicide Sheep, that is. For some reason best known to themselves, a mob of these stupid animals tried to throw themselves under our wheels. This happened to me once in Scotland, too, a couple of years later. Maybe it's me. After a break in the appropriately named Peace Hotel in Kandahar we were ready for the 1000km Dasht-i-Dargo, the Desert of Death.

Along the way we stopped for a swim in the Farrah River, the only

We found Afghan tea houses friendly and a welcome place of refreshment.

body of water between Kandahar and Herat. When we took the bikes down the river bank, a Desert of Death thorn lodged in Charlie's back tyre. When we were back in the mountains, it worked its way to the tube and caused a flat. We drank five litres of water each (the total contents of our water canisters) in the time it took to fix the first and then the second flat, which we caused when we disturbed an old patch. It was hot; in fact, it felt hotter than the 52 degrees we'd experienced in India. The only shade was inside a drain under the road, so that's where we did our second lot of repairs. I can see why they call it the Desert of Death.

Herat is an impressive town, with a more or less ruined fort in the middle and lots of other ruins around, as well as large, dusty but green parks. The electricity in Herat was a bit ... thin, I suppose. An American chap we met had been using a 110-volt shaver in the allegedly 240-volt sockets without trouble. The electricity wasn't the only thin thing in Herat. Our patience ran a bit thin, too, as we rushed around from one government office to the next trying to pay our fine for overstaying and getting exit permission.

The border was easy in comparison. We had been warned of people hiding drugs on our bikes and then reporting us, so we stopped short of the border and searched the bikes ourselves. Nothing. At the Afghani border post they didn't even search us.

CHAPTER 11

Iran

THE IRANIANS WERE A LITTLE keener. They seemed set to give us the sort of thorough going over a Land Rover was getting in the next parking bay. But then, when they brought out their bit of bent wire to probe the insides of our petrol tanks, I pointed out that they didn't need it. The plastic tanks were translucent and they could see that there was nothing inside. That impressed them so much they let us go on the spot. We left them prizing the lining out of the Land-Rover.

We made it to the holy city of Mashad's campsite and sat down to calm our nerves with a beer, our first encounter with Iranian drivers behind us. Iranians, I'm sorry to say, are the worst drivers in the world, or perhaps just the most fearless; even more than the Afghanis. They think nothing of pulling out to overtake a bus that's passing a truck that's passing another bus - on a blind corner. They are also unfamiliar with the use of the gears, or perhaps consider changing down an attack on their manhood. On flat roads, they drive in top gear with the accelerator flat to the boards and they don't change down for hills. As a result they were passing us on the flat and we were passing them as they were wheezing up the hills. This brought out the homicidal maniac in them, since it is apparently a deadly insult to pass a car on a bike. They would chase us and run us off the road. Consequently, we spent a great deal of time in the dirt, getting up the nerve to go back onto the tar. Every police station has a stone plinth outside with a particularly badly mangled car on it still bearing the blood stains of its collision, presumably as a warning. Nobody appears to take any notice.

> "The great religions are the ships, Poets the life boats. Every sane person I know has jumped overboard."
>
> **HAFIZ**

The primary mode of transport in Iran has not changed for a few centuries.

Very carefully we rode up to the Caspian Sea and then back down through a deep defile and over a beautiful pass to Tehran. In the evenings we camped with all the locals in the parks every town has on its outskirts, apparently solely for this purpose. The people who had been trying to kill us all day couldn't have been nicer; they helped us to find water, offered us tea and melon slices and gave us cigarettes. Then, the next morning, they went back to trying to kill us on the road.

Tehran traffic is so bad that we didn't even try to cope with it – we took the minibus to town from our campsite, the famous Gol-e-Sahra. Charlie managed to find some XL spares, including a new speedometer cable for mine. We also did some maintenance work. Then we decided to skip our planned excursion down to Esfahan - to be perfectly honest, I just refused to go – and headed straight for the border.

Our last camp in Iran was at Maku, behind the Maku Inn. It sticks in my mind because I managed to find some proper bread, thick and moist, a great treat after the dry stuff most Iranians eat. Once again people were most helpful and very friendly. I have nothing against the people in Iran – as long as they're not behind the wheel of a car.

At Maku we also met a couple of Swiss guys on XT500s fitted with 31-litre tanks. They were going to tackle the middle road through Afghanistan, which not only has no petrol stations but no road either. *Alles gute, Jungs.*

At the border, we buzzed past the enormous queue of TIR semitrailers waiting to be processed and got through the Iran side quickly and easily. Then we had to wait. There's a two-hour time change at the border and on the Turkish side it was not yet business hours. While we were waiting, we chatted to the people going the other way, who were mostly Germans going to jobs in Iran. They gave us helpful advice as well as a couple of gallons of petrol and a map of Turkey. There are so many nice people out there.

CHAPTER 12

Turkey

ONCE THE BORDER opened, we asked about insurance and were told that, yes, we had to have it. But the nearest place it was available was Erzurum, 200km to the west. Mmm. We rode off without it and nobody cared. At Dogubayazit - the locals call it 'Hozit, with rare good sense - we turned off the Asian Highway and headed up towards Kars. Although infested with cigarette cadgers and slightly longer, this road avoids the pass and the stretch of dirt road at Agri which I had not enjoyed six years before. The road wasn't bad at all despite a lot of gravel stretches and we spent the night at the rather nasty Pasinler Inn. Charlie was feeling unwell and went off to bed, and I had a major battle with the desk trying to change a traveller's cheque. Once they realised they wouldn't get paid if they didn't cash it, it was no problem.

Erzurum looked grim, and we didn't bother stopping for insurance.

> "*Be careful. The Turks can't drive, and they're crazy.*"
> **TURKISH TRUCK DRIVER**

It was exhausting getting to Trabzon on the Black Sea. The road was a fine example of the Turkish "too hard" syndrome. Wherever it ran over flat country it was tarred and in good repair; as soon as it approached one of the three passes and went up into the mountains it turned to dirt and deteriorated alarmingly. My theory is that it's easy to lay and fix flat roads, but mountains are too hard.

Lunch was at a little *lokanta* (bar or pub) in the hills, and a truck driver who had worked in Germany for a while, like so many of his countrymen, and spoke the language warned us about the other locals. "The Turks can't drive, and they're crazy," he said. They're not as bad as Iranians, Mustafa.

When we came over the last pass, we headed straight down into cloud and rain. It stayed with us until we left the Black Sea again. At the campsite in Trabzon we met an Australian couple in a Range-Rover who had just spent three weeks camped at a petrol station waiting for a delivery so they could fill their tank and go on. We carried every ounce of spare petrol we could from then on.

Scenery along the coast was pleasant enough but hardly stunning, and the constant drizzle dampened our spirits. This is where Xenophon's soldiers enthusiastically greeted the Black Sea as *"Thalatta! Thalatta!"* - "The sea! The sea!" but I couldn't get up much enthusiasm. Charlie, intrepid soul that he is, had a swim in it. We then struck the touring rider's bane - roadworks. There was mud on the road, and passing trucks threw up a fine film that settled on my spectacles and turned them opaque. Once out of that, we had a dice with a John Deere combine harvester; for once, we won. Back on the main cross-Turkey road, the traffic became a problem and I nearly killed myself when I misjudged the speed of a truck I was trying to pass.

Ankara was dreary and dirty, but the campsite was a welcome little

With Mount Ararat in the distance we try to avoid the Anatolian Plain's cigarette cadgers.

oasis. The guard looked like Rochester from the Jack Benny Show and refused to let us camp on the grass – we had to put up our shelter on the rocky verge. He also claimed to speak six languages, but they all turned out to be Turkish.

Our next destination was Cappadocia and the rock houses of Goreme, so we turned south. We rode past the salt Lake Tuz on good but monotonously straight roads down to Nevshehir and Goreme – there was a little trouble getting petrol but not much and we made it through without major delays.

"Paris Camping" supplied hot showers on our first night, but then we moved down to the Rock House Hotel which was much more "authentic". Some enterprising local souls had laid down a few carpets in one of the old stone houses and had turned it into an hotel. It was not exactly luxury class – the bathroom consisted of a puddle halfway up the hill and the toilets were the surrounding vineyards – but it was cheap and interesting. We pottered around for a couple of days looking at the truly amazing carving – what could be more amazing than a whole village of carved houses – and then continued south towards the coast.

Just out of Nigde, the spring clip holding the rear wheel spacer on Charlie's bike gave out. In one of the neatest pieces of open-road surgery I have ever seen, he fabricated a new clip by hacksawing a piece out of the spare spacer from Penang and bending it together. A good man to have along is Charlie.

We buzzed down through the ferocious traffic in the Cilician Gates, the main pass leading to the Middle East, and had a lunch of expensive half-raw roast chicken in Mersin. I demonstrated my masculinity (or stupidity) by eating an entire large hot pepper and lost, I estimate, a kilo with all the sweat that poured out of me.

We regretted our decision to spend the night in the grandiose BP Mocamp at Silifke, too – the allegedly hot showers were cold and the staff must have been specially selected for insolence. And it was expensive.

Things improved after that, with the road becoming more

interesting as the coast became more rugged. It's pretty country, and campsites jump out at you from under the pine trees – unofficial campsites. We spent one night high up in the hills sitting around a fire and feeling thoroughly at peace with the world.

A quick look at the famous Crusader castle at Anamur and a dip in the Med prepared us for another day on the road, although it didn't prepare us for the couple we met driving a camper van with an "Australia" sticker on the back. I'd gone to school with Alex, and Charlie had gone to University with Carol's brother. Do you want to say it or shall I? Small world, ain't it...

In Antalya they were tarring both sides of the main road and the detour through the lanes wasn't signposted. We saw every back street in that town at least twice before we got out. Then we came across a chilling sight – row upon row of little asbestos-sheet huts on the beach, behind barbed wire. We thought it was a concentration camp, but it turned out to be a holiday village.

The Kemer road was pretty again, with pine forests and cliffs and a little cafe under the trees by a waterfall. But our nemesis, road works, struck again and we struggled through bulldozed mudbaths to Kas. This picturesque little fishing village lies at the foot of a 300m cliff, is very attractive but lacks a campground, so exploring along the dirt track that pretends to be a main road west of here we found a sheltered beach where we could set up camp.

Charlie's bike was beginning to worry us now. It was difficult to start and had begun to leak oil badly around the head gasket. Doing the timing didn't improve things and it became obvious that two of the head bolts had stripped the thread in the barrel.

After a glass of tea at dozy Kalkhan we tackled the gravel section we'd heard of. It was interesting, all right. I took it at speed and unusually got so far ahead that Charlie turned around to see if he hadn't passed me without realising it. After we got together again, my bike went into a terrifying tank slapper at about 80km/h. I'll say this, I didn't fall off. No thanks to my riding ability; I just hung on, and I think I screamed. Then Charlie was very nearly skittled by a tractor that turned across the road in front of him. But the people were nice to us, gave us vegetables and let us camp on their land.

A short but scary run with the traffic on the main road, the E23, took us to Istanbul and over the great new toll bridge to Europe. At the Youth Hostel near the Blue Mosque our bikes once again found a home in the lobby. Istanbul traffic looks quite terrifying, but isn't all that bad on a bike. We met a couple of sad-looking blokes at the post office who had been waiting for the third member of their party for two days. On the way out of town, he and his 650 Yamaha had disappeared. These two were leaning on their BMW and Honda 500 twin hoping he'd turn up. As they were headed for Australia they still had quite a way to go.

We went for a ferry trip on the Bosphorus, ate hugely at a little snack bar specialising in shish kebabs, shopped at the Grand Bazaar and even sampled the nightlife. In one bar a Turkish seaman who had been to Australia insisted on buying us beers. When we finally demurred because we had to ride back to the hostel, he looked at us unbelievingly and said, "What kind of Australians are you?"

Southwest Turkey is mild and pleasant, a relief after all the deserts.

Finally we left for the Greek border. Then Charlie's bike misbehaved again, spluttering and refusing to pull. For those of you who can no longer stand the suspense, it was the timing. It was checked later with a strobe and found to be way out. So don't try to do static timing on an XL, OK?

The border was boring. But then, very few borders aren't, and I'd rather have a boring one anyway. Excitement at borders generally means trouble.

CHAPTER 13

Greece

IN GREECE, AS IN Turkey, they write your bike into your passport so you can't sell it and disrupt the local economy. If, on your way out, you can't produce the bike, they don't let you leave. With this in mind, and knowing that Charlie would be flying out to attend a genetics congress in Moscow, we asked Customs to write both bikes into my passport. As I would be looking after them until Charlie came back, that seemed reasonable.

Not to Customs it didn't. First they were very suspicious of this trip to Moscow, which Charlie had unfortunately mentioned. Was he going off to get instructions from the Kremlin? Then they decided it was against the law to bring in more than one bike on one passport. Then the bank at the border wouldn't sell us any petrol coupons. Bikes didn't entitle us to them.

Our first impressions of Greece were sorted out over a lunch of calamari and retsina in Alexandropoulis, and we weren't sure we liked it. After the third bottle of retsina we mellowed, and that night in Kavala we decided it wasn't such a bad place. We spent the evening sitting at a sidewalk cafe, listening to a trio with two clarinetty things and a bass drum playing something that didn't sound in the least like "Zorba", and had a few beers. Then we dossed down in the vineyards and slept under the stars.

> "*Greece is not an easy country to do business in.*"
> ALI BABACAN

We couldn't quite work out what was happening in Thessalonica. There were tents everywhere, in parks, squares, even in parking lots. A Boy Scout convention? No, it turned out that there had been an earthquake and nobody was game to go back into their houses. No wonder. Greek building codes are honoured far more in the breach than in the observance. We had one building pointed out to us that had begun with three stories, but now had six – one added on at a time, ad hoc.

Around this area bike cops abounded, mounted on machines as varied as Nortons, Moto Guzzis, BMWs and, of course, old Harley-Davidson Glides. The local bikers seemed to favour the mighty 50cc Kreidler Florett.

Time was running out – Charlie's congress started the next week – so we found ourselves a campsite down on the Halkidiki peninsula and settled in.

I wrote to Annie, who was then supposed to be in Athens. Charlie went through all the Customs hassles that we had hoped to avoid, putting his bike into bond so that they would cross it out of his passport. The bond turned out to be an underground car-park. He even had to pay the parking fee when he came back.

Once alone, I settled into a happy routine involving eating, sleeping and visits to the taverna, with a bit of swimming thrown in. Annie arrived, looking edible in her Chicago Bears T-shirt, and we spent an idyllic week together. She had to go back and start her Eurail pass

The Greeks know a good bit of mechanical engineering when they see it.

then, and Charlie returned. He had his tent, which an obliging fellow scientist had brought all the way from Australia. He also had a box of genuine Havana cigars and a bottle of Russian vodka, with which we celebrated his return in style.

New tyres, East German semi-trials pattern, went onto the bikes and we moved to Thessalonica to get something done about the stripped threads in Charlie's cylinder. He had spotted a shop advertising helicoiling. The mechanic took a look at the bike and nodded, sure, he could helicoil that. Then he retapped it to a larger bolt size. What happened to the helicoiling, we asked. Helicoiling? Oh, helicoiling. They didn't do that, any more. We went and had another beer. The bolts worked fine.

CHAPTER 14

Yugoslavia

YUGOSLAVIA LOOKED great at first. Even the autoput, famous for its state of disrepair, was in pretty good nick. On the first night we hid away in a bit of forest, since free camping is not allowed in this country, and set up the tent. The rain started early in the morning, and it became obvious to me as we rode up into the dripping hillside forest before Prizren that my wet weather gear was due for retirement.

Just after Pec, the alleged main road turned into a gravel path, then a goat track and then it started crawling up and down an endless procession of ridges. It got colder, it got wetter, and I became more and more miserable. Charlie was at least dry! The bikes handled the "road" quite well, but I'd hate to do that stretch on anything but a trail bike. I'd hate to do it again on a trail bike!

> *"Better to be an honourable man than a Minister of State."*
> **MILOVAN DJILAS**

We stopped under an overhang to consider whether this could possibly be the main road. The driver of a battered locally-built Fiat that came along assured us that it was, giving us the left-fist-in-the air and right-hand-on-left-biceps salute to show us how tough he thought we were. I hope that's what he meant, anyway. We headed back out into the cold rain.

A tiny pub saved us, high up on a ridge top. It provided brandy and hot bean soup, and it was warm. The scenery was chocolate-box pretty, and not much later the road improved as well. The last few miles to Titograd weren't bad at all and we saw lots of other bikes, mainly touring BMWs with German plates. The Titograd campground had the loveliest lady at reception and hot showers. We camped under the damp trees and, feeling human after the shower, went over to the restaurant for some dinner.

Since there was a "music charge" if you ate in the main restaurant, we settled for sitting with the help in the kitchen and listened to the strains of "Ramona" and "Charmaine" filtering through the door, for free.

The Kotor hill with its hairpins, rotten surface and steep drop impressed us greatly, as did the tour buses using it at breakneck speed. There was another cloudburst just after we left Kotor Bay and we arrived sodden in Dubrovnik. There was even water in our panniers, a most unusual occurrence. We splurged on a pension to dry out. The pension made a good base for exploring the old walled city. We wandered around the steep stone paths, admired the medieval buildings and splurged once more, this time on a top-notch meal. Despite the heavy emphasis on tourism, Dubrovnik seemed a pleasant place to us. A pity that most of the tourists were so dull and conservatively dressed. The few Americans made a pleasant splash of colour with their bright T-shirts and Bermuda shorts.

We had clear sky and sun most of the way up the coast. The hills are quite stark here, dry and infertile and the limestone ranges look as though they've been hit with a gigantic mallet and shattered. This is an early example of the dangers of clear-felling. The Romans cut down all the trees, around the time of Christ or before, and the country has never recovered. The goats which were introduced subsequently helped by eating anything green. Jagged rocks are everywhere, and we had trouble finding a flat place large enough to put up the tent. We finally settled on the concrete base of a building that had never been constructed.

CHAPTER 15

Italy

"I think people in Italy live their lives better than we do... they've learned to celebrate dinner and lunch, whereas we sort of eat as quickly as we can to get through it."

GEORGE CLOONEY

COMING UP TO THE Italian border, the temporary circlip Charlie had made in Turkey broke again. He had to use one of the spacers fitted to the bike to make another, which led to a great deal of play in the rear wheel. We jumped the two-mile queue at the border – motorbikes are invaluable for that – and got as far as Trieste. No, signore, XLs are not imported into Italy. So there were no spares. What now? The bike was pretty well unridable in its present state, and eventually the rear wheel would of course fall off. Charlie, being an incurable optimist, decided we should make some spacers out of a spare inner tube. Being a decidedly curable optimist, I pointed out that Soichiro Honda would hardly make spacers out of steel if rubber would do the job just as well.

Unfortunately I was right. The bike ate the rubber spacers on the autostrada. We got the can opener out and made some more out of the tops of oil cans. Did you know that they use really thin metal for oil cans? We made dozens of infinitely thin oil can top spacers and hobbled along, periodically making more until the hopelessness of that solution finally sank in. We camped in a layby near Vicenza and slept with our heads inches from the traffic roaring past. A bike shop came to our rescue in the morning; they turned a new, thick spacer and fitted a new circlip, and we had no more trouble. I was so grateful that I bought a set of rainproof overalls from them.

Cheered by all this success, we decided to get an idea of the real Italy by taking the back roads. After a number of suicide attempts under our wheels we returned to the autostrada at Verona. Italy was a bit too hectic. Tolls weren't expensive for bikes on the autostrada and we buzzed along in fine style, passing Milan's enormous suburbs and turning up into the Alps. We forgot to use our last petrol coupons at the last station in Italy. Anyone have a use for a 10-litre Italian petrol coupon?

CHAPTER 16

Switzerland

THERE WAS A LITTLE hut at the border selling Green Card insurance, so we finally weakened and bought some. Of course, no one asked for it when we crossed. Our camp that night was right on the lake at Lugano, comfortable and quiet, and a pleasant change from the previous night almost literally on the Autostrada.

I made one of my famous navigational mistakes the next morning. We had a choice between the St Bernhard tunnel and the St Gotthard Pass, and I thought: "Who wants to spend such a lovely day underground?"

So up into the Alps we went, past the trucks cleaning the roadside gravel (it's true! they do, in Switzerland) until it started to drizzle. With wet-weather gear on, we continued. The drizzle turned to snow, and we were still nowhere near the top. Instead of turning around like sensible people we pressed on and finally made the pass in the driving snow. We were not exactly dressed for this kind of weather, and had even disposed of our visors some time before because they had become too scratched to be safe. Ice formed on our beards and my glasses. I have never been so cold in my life.

> "When you're dealing with Switzerland... it's best to keep one thing in mind. Switzerland is not a real country. It's a business, and it's run like a business."
>
> DANIEL SILVA

On top of all this, the Swiss have a charming habit of cutting parallel grooves in the road surface. No doubt this is useful in preventing cars from sliding all over the place in snow, but it imparts a weave to small motorcycles that is distinctly unsettling. Or would be if I had had any time spare from being cold to be unsettled. A welcome pub supplied coffee and brandy once we were below the snow line on the other side, and we continued to Zurich in the driving rain.

What the hell, it was only rain...

The border with Germany was complicated. Our road first crossed to Germany, then back to Switzerland and then back to Germany again, all in the space of about 16km. It was lucky that we had bought Green Cards in Italy, because this time everybody wanted to see them. The Germans also pored over all the exotic stamps in our passports for a while and I thought they might decide to search us. But no, they'd just been curious.

CHAPTER 17

Germany and beyond

IT WAS THE MIDDLE OF September by now, and Germany was quite cold. We slept in our clothes that night and the next. On the second evening, we found a pub which looked convivial and asked if there was a campground within walking distance. Always get your priorities right.

"Yes," said the bloke behind the bar. "But it is perhaps a dozen steps," and pointed at the orchard next to the pub. "It is also free, but only," and he lifted a finger, "if you drink here."

Charlie discovered the uniquely German tradition of the Stammtisch when he attempted to sit at it. In most if not all country pubs, the Stammtisch is reserved for regulars - and off limits to everyone else. It was no big deal, but an interesting introduction to a country where rules are rules. Charlie also discovered that bakeries usually served coffee as well, something that has become common in Australia but wasn't then. We both approved.

After a long day on the autobahn, we arrived in Brunswick and my aunt and uncle made us welcome. They fed us up for a few days and my aunt dropped our clothes into the washing machine. We couldn't believe that it was actually possible to get the stuff clean again. At lunchtime, my aunt produced what she knew was one of my favourite sandwich toppings: raw pork with salt and minced onions. I have to give Charlie top marks here; he overcame a lifetime of Australian conditioning and tried it - and even liked it.

> *"Besides Germany, the only countries that don't have speed limits are places like Nepal, where road conditions are so bad that a limit would be beside the point."*
> **SIGMAR GABRIEL**

We visited more relatives in Luneburg and Hamburg and then rode over to Amersfoort in Holland to stay a night with Frank, the Harley rider we'd met in Penang. A marvelous evening followed, recounting woes and laughing about mishaps. All very easy to do afterwards.

After crossing Belgium in something like an hour, we turned down towards Paris. The autoroute is quite expensive, and you can't get a glass of wine in the restaurants – in France of all places! Our friends in Paris, Campbell of BMW R60 fame and Renee, were away for the weekend. We camped at the big campsite in the Bois and had a look at the famous city. When they returned we moved over to their flat and spent a few days being deluged with French hospitality.

Campbell wanted to go over to London to buy a bike, so when the time came we offered him a lift. The bikes looked like overloaded camels as we transferred some of my load to Charlie and Campbell crouched behind me. We still made good time to Boulogne, through the rain, but then the hovercraft didn't want us. No bikes allowed on Seaspeed. We took the normal ferry and actually had a dry road from Dover to London. Just out of Dover we passed an elderly bearded man in a shalwar kameez. Campbell dug me in the ribs and shouted, "Now I know we're in England, there's an Englishman!"

CHAPTER 18

England, Wales and Ireland

"When money's tight and it's hard to get
And your horse has also ran,
When all you have is a heap of debt –
A pint of plain is your only man.

FLANN O'BRIEN

I BOUGHT SOME NEW wet-weather gear and we took off again, into a headwind to Wales and the lovely hills above Swansea. Then Charlie's throttle cable broke. We had a spare, so it didn't matter, did it? But the spare turned out to be a return cable, which is not interchangeable with the actuating one. Only Honda design engineers know why.

Kevin and Skippy, a young Welsh couple, came to our assistance. Skippy got her name from the fact that she'd spent some time in Australia as a child. They showed me a bike shop where I secured a new cable and then invited us over to their place. We spent the evening in the weirdest pub I have ever seen, the walls covered in comic book characters, and enjoyed ourselves drinking a lethal beer called Colt 45.

Welsh roads were as much fun as Welsh people, and our enjoyment of the ride was only spoiled by mysterious headaches the next morning. The crossing from Fishguard was uneventful, except that they sprayed us with disinfectant when we rolled ashore in Rosslare. With both bikes running noticeably rough now, we spent a few days exploring the south of Ireland, especially enjoying the Ring of Kerry and a priceless bed-and-breakfast place in Portroe.

This was where we heard the wonderful story of the elderly couple, holidaying in Portroe, who had been kept awake long into the night by some of the local boys fanging about on their bikes. In the morning they went to the Garda, the police, and complained, "What do you think about people riding loud motorcycles around town all night?" The Garda looked at him for a while and then replied, "As long as it's just the two of you I suppose it will be all right..."

On to Dublin and a hero's welcome at the Guinness Brewery, where they poured untold quantities of the precious fluid down our throats (including the rare and lethal XXX), stood us a truly magnificent lunch and had us interviewed for radio and papers. Laden with gifts, we retired to our B&B and tried to come to terms with the fact that the trip, for now, was over. Just as well we were in Dublin. It's hard to get depressed in a place with so many good pubs.

We both returned to England and settled in London for a while. Charlie worked as a despatch rider, possibly the only one with a PhD (then again, possibly not) and I met up with Annie and got a job first in an advertising agency and then a publishing firm. It was almost like normal life...

The gate of the Guinness Brewery, a welcome sight as we reached the other Dublin.

PART 2
Three Continent Diversion

CHAPTER 19

France

SCROLL FORWARD SIX OR EIGHT MONTHS. Annie and I had now enjoyed one winter in Britain, and didn't want to face another. So the plans were made – we would go to North Africa for the coming cold months. Yamaha Germany very kindly offered us an XS1100 on loan, and we snapped it up. It was taken down to Vetter Industries and fitted with a Windjammer fairing as well as panniers and a top box, turning it into the closest thing to a one-bike invasion force I had ever seen.

Neil and Millie, another Australian couple, decided to join us on their Suzuki GS750. This was fitted with a sports sidecar by Squire and the roomy luggage from Craven; Boyers also fitted their electronic ignition. None of us had camping gear for more than the odd long weekend, so we spent a morning with the folk at Binleys Camping Supplies in Kettering and staggered out fully equipped. We were also sponsored by Everoak Helmets, by Derriboots, Nivea and by Duckham's Oils. Thanks, all, once again.

> *"If the path be beautiful, ask not where it leads."*
> **ANATOLE FRANCE**

It had taken a fair bit of work to get sponsorship, but a well-produced proposal and a carefully thought out set of benefits for the sponsors (mentions like this one) swung the odds in our favour, and we got just about everything we asked for. Mind you, the Yamaha, its fairing and luggage and the Suzuki's sidecar had to be given back after the trip.

At the beginning of November, badly overloaded and not really fully prepared, we rolled aboard the ferry to France. It was dark when we reached Le Havre, but we had little trouble finding the campground. Not that it did us much good for, just four days earlier, the site had closed for the season. We set up camp in the park across the road, dined on sandwiches we'd made from the remaining contents of our

Annie enjoys the rays of the morning sun above Ghardaia in Algeria.

refrigerator before leaving London, and slept very well. I always sleep better when it's free...

The road signs and our maps were rather confusing in the morning, so although we had intended to follow the byroads to Paris we ended up on the autoroute. It was Sunday and the road was full of pretty bikes, all sharp and clean, and we felt rather out of place lumbering along on our overloaded camels.

The Bois de Boulogne campsite extended its usual welcome, with deep mud and inoperative showers. It's not all bad, really. There are a lot of trees and it's quite close to the centre of the city. I do wish they'd fix those showers. About half of them just swallow your token, burp and give you nothing in return. Most of the others give you your few minutes of hot water, but there's always one that's stuck "on" and therefore free. The procedure, therefore, is never to go into an unoccupied cubicle. Wait until somebody comes out of one and ask "*C'est marche?*" before committing your token. If one shower has a queue in front of it, that's the free one. Wait for that.

If all the above sounds like too much trouble, imagine the

Fully sponsored and loaded, ready for departure from Telegraph Hill, London.

frustration of getting undressed, putting your token in the slot without being rewarded with hot water, getting dressed, plodding over to the office to complain and get another token, getting undressed, putting your token... In 1979 the showers had been like that for at least eleven years, to my knowledge.

It rained during the night, and the top of the Lowrider tent Neil and Millie were using filled up with water, but surprisingly little seeped through. Neil and I spent the next day working on the bikes, finishing all the little things we should have done back in London. Some people from a minibus camped next door wandered over and gave us the wonderful news that they'd just come back from Morocco and it had rained all the time.

After dinner, I found reassurance in a sip of my duty-free Glenfiddich and we once again donned our Damart gear to go to bed. It was cold enough to penetrate our down sleeping bags. A few days in Paris were fun, but the rain refused to let up and we pushed on towards the Mediterranean.

One of the alterations we had made to the GS was fitting it with GS1000 air shocks. As we rolled out of Paris, these proved to be underinflated, and as we could not work out how to get more air into them without losing oil, we changed back to the old units. A wet day followed, with occasional glimpses of the lovely French autumn countryside as we rolled through the forests. We had a picnic at lunchtime – in an old disused petrol station at Sens. It was the only place we could get in out of the rain.

Somewhat further along and after dark, I switched the XS onto high beam coming out of a tunnel and promptly blew a fuse. A few hectic seconds followed – there was a corner somewhere out there – before I'd stopped safely on the gravel. The original 10-amp fuse was obviously not enough to cope with the extra load of all the lights the Vetter gear features, so I replaced it with a 22-amp one and had no further trouble.

What a ride! In the three days it took us to make our way down to the Med, we discovered just about all of the defects our equipment was to show during the entire trip. The Vetter panniers leaked a little, and tightening the locks only cured one. To be fair, Vetter told us later that our panniers had come from the only less than perfect batch they'd had. The sidecar hood wasn't entirely waterproof either, and the occupant complained that it was a little claustrophobic. The GS battery refused to hold a charge and the XS happily followed every white line that presented itself. At one point I had to make a crash stop on the outfit, and the overloaded sidecar pulled me into the opposing lane, fortunately without dire results. At least the fairings proved their value; the Windjammer was excellent and even the little Corsair on the GS helped a lot in the rain.

Tempers wore a bit thin, too. Luckily we found good campsites all the way. One night somewhere near Lyon we even found a free flat. We had pulled up to ask someone about a campsite when they told us to follow them and took us to a half-empty block of flats. They shooed us into one of them and said goodnight. There wasn't much furniture, but it was warm and dry.

It was a great relief to find some sun – not much, but some – in Marseille. We camped at La Ciotat after a run along the coast road, where we had another chance to admire the local bikes. Mostly kitted out as endurance racers, they all seemed to be piloted by riders bent on suicide. They were fun to watch. Our spirits were restored by an excellent if horrendously expensive bouillabaisse, which we consumed with great gusto. Like Charlie's and my French dinner in Chieng Mai, in Thailand, it was a great morale booster for all of us.

We spent a few evenings in the "Civette du Port", a friendly little bar where we fascinated the waiters by playing Scrabble late into the night. Our campsite wasn't very pleasant, and it was still so cold that we slept in our thermal wear every night. A short run to St Tropez wasn't terribly impressive, either. The coast road is plastered with "Private Property" signs forbidding picnics, camping and even stopping. Ah, vive la France, sure.

Renewed sunshine cheered us up again and we set off west along the coast in fine spirits. But France really didn't seem to be for us. Just past Marseilles, the GS suddenly developed a very flat tyre. Inspection showed four broken spokes, one of which had punctured the tube. The overloading was taking its toll. Neil and I respoked the wheel as well as we could beside the road, patched the tube and limped to the nearest campsite at Carry Le Rouet.

As if that last mishap had been the parting shot from our evil luck, things began to look up immediately. The campsite was comfortable and had excellent hot showers; a bike shop in Marseilles respoked the wheel for us in a couple of hours; and the mistral started to blow the rain clouds out to sea. I did get lost on the way back from the bike shop, admittedly, and saw most of southern France before I got back onto the proper autoroute....

A major sort-out followed and we sent three large, heavy parcels back home. My typewriter went, too – sadly missed; I hate writing longhand, and there were no laptops then! Then we loaded most of the remaining heavy gear aboard the XS which hardly seemed to feel the difference. We were all breathing more easily as we buzzed off along the coast, over the classy motorway bridge at Martigues and on

Re-spoking the rear wheel of the Suzuki by the side of the road.

to Arles for an excellent lunch.

It is difficult to imagine how such flat countryside can be so beautiful, but the Camargue, with its waterways, stands of golden reeds and herds of white horses, looked lovely. With the mistral at our backs, we drifted through the meadows and occasional stands of umbrella pine down to Les Saintes Maries with its little chapel that attracts thousands of Gypsy pilgrims every year. The town centre still felt quite medieval with its winding alleys and little shops, but a huge modern holiday development all around rather spoils it.

In the sandy campsite we did a little more maintenance work on the bikes and I couldn't understand why it was impossible to get the rear brake disc of the XS back between the calipers after I had replaced the pads. Lots of headscratching later, it occurred to me that I'd refilled the brake fluid reservoir as well. Sure enough, I'd put in too much fluid. The spokes on the GS seemed to be holding. We tapped them every day now.

There was still aggravation in our little party as personalities clashed, and Annie and I took the opportunity to spend a couple of

Rural France can be quite idyllic, especially along the extensive canal network.

evenings by ourselves in a comfortable bar by the harbour, drinking kir and gazing into the fire. The bar mascot, a dachshund, kept us company. He had a very simple way of indicating that the fire was getting too low - he would crawl right up into the brick fireplace and look out mournfully.

We moved camp after some days of this rather heavily touristed environment; our new home was "La Refuge", a tiny place in the town of Vias. On the way, Neil once more puzzled the locals by asking where the war was when he meant the railway station. His rather good French always seemed to fail him when he had to differentiate between "*gare*" and "*guerre*".

We also met a young German woman on a Honda 400/4, who calmly informed us that she was going down to The Gambia to sell her bike. Carrying very little gear, she had been freezing in her leathers for the last three days. We gave her some lunch and wished her luck.

Vias proved to be exactly what we needed - it was just a small wine and tourist village in the off season. With friendly people and the "Cafe de France", where we became such good customers that the patron started buying us drinks, the place was cosy. If truth be known the free drinks were a result of his being unable to tell the difference between Australia and New Zealand. Every time we walked in he would burst into a big grin and say admiringly, "Ah, les All Blacks!"

We had a couple of barbecues on the beach and generally took it easy. Our bail bond insurance for Spain didn't start for another eight days. I also had new tyres, Metzelers, fitted to the XS at the Honda shop in Beziers. The rear wheel nearly reduced their mechanics to tears, and it took them three times as long as they'd quoted to replace the tyre. They swore they would never touch another XS 1100. I still don't know why; I've replaced a rear tyre on that bike myself and it gave me very little trouble.

Feeling more relaxed, we continued to Biarritz via Toulouse. A sunny morning and pleasant lunch at the very beautiful mediaeval town of Carcassonne were followed by a freezing, impenetrable fog just outside Toulouse. With our heated handlebar grips, electric

GloGloves and Motomod Alaskan suits we weren't exactly cold – but we still couldn't see. A campsite loomed out of the fog just in time.

Our flysheets were frozen stiff the next morning, and we had to thaw them out in the toilet block before we could fold them. The fog was still as dense as the night before. We crept through Toulouse, visibility a few metres. To this day I have no idea what the place looks like.

An hour later, the fog lifted and we had the sunniest day of the trip so far. Our run that day through the hills of Gascony was nothing short of idyllic. This was the home of cassoulet, Armagnac and foie gras, substantial chalets peering out of the little copses, and the snowy slopes of the Pyrenees blinking away on the horizon. I kept seeing signs all day advertising "Chiens Bergers Allemandes" and my mind kept twisting the translation to German Dogburgers, possibly competition for the American fast food chains. They were only selling German Shepherds, of course.

In a little village just before our camp at St Sever, we passed a small church called Notre Dame du Rugby. Now that's taking sports to heart.

St Sever is on the edge of the Gironde and lies peacefully in a

In the morning in Toulouse, our tents were frozen into hard sheets.

wooded valley. Our petrol stove was acting up, giving only a low flame when it would burn at all. We consoled ourselves with a few drinks in the bar/tobacconist/newsagents/shop in the village. Even this out-of-the-way place had an electronic amusement machine, featuring little clowns breaking balloons. I was interested to see that the last "human" score had been twenty, while the clowns by themselves often racked up 30-35. Clever little electronic clowns....

It was cold again that night, but not unpleasant, and the next day we were nearly at Biarritz when the back wheel of the GS collapsed once more. Oh dear.

We located a Suzuki shop in Bayonne, but they claimed they couldn't help until the next day. When we pointed out that this meant our sleeping by the side of the road, they gave us the name of another shop in Biarritz. After much pleading, the chap there agreed to rebuild the wheel for us, but he didn't think there were any heavier spokes available. We had to face facts. There was little point in laying out more money when the spokes would only break again. We had to buy a cast wheel.

After an elaborate series of phone calls, our friend in the bike shop arranged for the other shop to stay open for us and to accept traveller's cheques. Neil raced back to Bayonne, bought the wheel, raced back to Biarritz, had it fitted with our wheel bearings, tyre and tube; and we put the wheel back on the bike. By now it was nearly 10 pm, and we had a great deal of trouble finding an open campground. Tempers flared. When we did find a site, we agreed that we must talk our frictions out.

Annie and I spent a relaxing day in Biarritz, where we picked up mail and had a picnic out on the beachfront rocks. Then we all got together for our bit of group therapy in one of the local bars. It emerged that Annie and I didn't really think that Millie could cope with this kind of travelling, and that she found me too bossy and overbearing. We thought she complained and niggled too much; she thought we didn't listen to her enough. We adjourned after a bit of healthy self-criticism, and things did improve quite noticeably for a while.

CHAPTER 20

Spain

We crossed into Spain with minimal formalities and followed an awful, pockmarked road to San Sebastian. We stuck it out for long enough to buy a gas stove with a little bottle and then took to the hills. While the road didn't improve, the air at least became transparent again. The pollution was grim.

We rode through some lovely autumn hill country to Pamplona, which was all rather spoilt by the amount of waste plastic hanging from riverside trees. There were fun and games in Pamplona, with our blue Australian passports acting like the proverbial red rag to a bull. Every time we showed them at any of the pensions, they were suddenly and mysteriously full. It was later explained to us that Australians have a bad name for their behavior during the running of the bulls. The boys must really have misbehaved to upset the Spaniards that badly!

> *"I would sooner be a foreigner in Spain than in most countries. How easy it is to make friends in Spain!"*
> **GEORGE ORWELL**

We had to find somewhere to stay, because the campsites were all closed for the season and it was getting late. Finally someone relented, tricked only a little bit by being shown Neil's British passport first. But Neil and I had to share one room and the girls another, under the watchful eye of a shawl-draped crone. It appears there's this law...

The bikes stayed out in the street, chained to a lamp post and to each other, with their alarms on. Dire warnings of bike theft had made us paranoid. An old gentleman told us that we were "loco" to leave them there, but he couldn't offer an alternative. We went to do the bars and had a great evening. There was no need to go to a restaurant – the bars all served tapas, delicious snacks such as liver with onions, pork and pimentos and grilled sardines, all of which we washed down with glasses of the cheap vino tinto. We were hardly

You hardly notice that you're changing continents on the Virgin of Africa.

incognito, however. Wherever we went in town, we were greeted with cries of "*Inglese moto!*"

The bikes were still there the next morning. They weren't entirely untouched - someone had carefully peeled most of the stickers off them.

Breakfast was by the side of the road as we had a long way to go that day. It consisted of jam on fresh bread bought from a van and coffee heated on our new gas stove. A great improvement over the petrol stove - it took less than half as long.

It was a long grind for the rest of the day, 12 hours down to the coast at Vinaroz, near Barcelona. The Ebro valley is flat and agricultural and there was a great deal of mist, which hid anything that might have been worth seeing. Just before the coast, up in some hills and in the dark, we passed Morello and were spooked by the chill bulk of the castle hulking over the town. Had there been a lighted tower window, I could well have imagined a latter-day vampire sitting down to . . . err . . . breakfast.

Castel Camping offered another castle, albeit a fake one built out of concrete blocks, and iron-hard ground. The hard ground turned out to be a common feature in Spain. Take heavy-duty pegs if you go. The grounds were deserted when we arrived, but the owners, a German couple, returned from a night at the movies just as we were setting up. They were friendly, turned on the hot water for us, and we all went to bed - very tired.

A little maintenance work the next day was interrupted by the arrival of a German tour bus. Its occupants spent the day in the site restaurant, listening to salesmen who were demonstrating kitchen gadgets. I couldn't contain my curiosity, and during their lunch break I asked what was going on. It appeared that they got a free bus from (and back to) Germany in exchange for sitting down and listening to the sales pitch. Funny way to spend your holidays.

The coast south to Valencia was dreary and dirty. Every lay-by seems to be used as a rubbish dump, the rivers are open sewers and it's dull country. Valencia does have a good market and that, combined

Annie rolls out of the campsite in Seville aboard the Suzuki.

with the ridiculously cheap booze, reconciled me to the place. Our campsite was south of the city and surrounded by blocks of "holiday flats". We had a little potato bake on the beach and consumed a few litres of Sangria, but we felt as though we were being watched by the brooding, empty-eyed concrete giants all around us.

Dreadful hangovers in the morning made packing a bit of a chore. Then, back on the road, both Neil and I kept imagining there was something wrong with the bikes – it was just Sangria withdrawal symptoms. But we certainly didn't imagine the bottle that burst on the pavement near us when we stopped to cash a cheque. I guess someone in the apartment block behind us didn't like bikes; they certainly had a very graphic way of showing it. We moved. The Costa del Fish 'n' Chips rolled past, looking grimmer than a suburb of Calcutta, and we camped in an excruciatingly expensive site near Alicante. Spanish campsites do not offer off season rates like the French ones, and they're out to squeeze every peseta they can out of you. Nasty places.

It did become interesting, and more pleasant, after we had crossed the Sierra Nevada to Granada. A cosy campsite made up for the fact that we'd arrived on the Feast of the Immaculate Conception and everything was closed. The Alhambra was worth looking at, although it can hardly compete with some of the great buildings in the same style in India or Pakistan. The Red Fort at Delhi, for instance, is both more intricate and grandiose. Unlike Delhi Granada does, however, boast good pastry shops, which we explored at leisure. Annie had what we assumed was an allergy reaction and her hands became itchy and covered in a rash. Antihistamine cream and tablets helped, but she had a great deal of difficulty sleeping. I think it had something to do with the amount of chlorine in the water.

On the way to Seville we passed quite a number of bike cops in pairs on their pitiful Sanglas 500s. A couple of them found it difficult to disguise their envy of the Yamaha when we pulled up, but tried to act nonchalant.

Coming into Seville was a little like coming home. There are large stands of gum trees and casuarinas, both natives of Australia, but while the orange trees that line the streets look fine from a distance, the polluted air has done its work and close up the fruit is grey, the leaves crippled. There was the most glorious cathedral, though, with buttress upon buttress reaching out from the nave until it all looked like a cross between an enormous centipede and an equally huge spider.

CHAPTER 21

Portugal

THE PORTUGUESE BORDER was next, through mountain ranges hung with mist and covered in cork oaks. The road was awful, like most Spanish roads, but offered pretty surroundings for a change. The undergrowth was inhabited by troops of pigs snuffling around for fallen acorns. Portuguese Customs checked our papers quite thoroughly, but gave us no trouble. The road just over the border was even worse than the ones in Spain, and for a while I held an image in my mind of us limping into Lisbon with totally ruined shock absorbers. But lo! Within a mile or so the surface became quite reasonable and stayed that way through most of the country. We spent that night in the municipal campsite at Beja, a green and cheerful place that cost us a tenth of what the last site in Spain had. Things were looking up.

I took us on a tour of rural Portugal the next day when I confused the road signs, but no one minded. The road went through forests with the occasional village squatting in its fields. Our first major town held a surprise. This was Setubal, which has the most diabolical one-way system known to man. It is necessary to traverse just about every street in town before emerging at the other side. I hit a pothole, too, that I thought was going to swallow the bike whole.

> *"Love one another and you will be happy; it is as simple and as difficult as that."*
> **PORTUGUESE PROVERB**

From the south, Lisbon is approached by a long, high suspension bridge. Neil, who was riding the XS, noticed that the bridge had no guard rail, and the gusty wind kept blowing him over to the side, and he didn't enjoy that at all.

You'd never have any trouble finding the campsite in Lisbon. It's so well signposted that you'd think the city was an adjunct to the site rather than the other way around. A pleasure to not have to search for ages, just for a change. Lisbon itself turned out to be a homely sort of place, with good shops and pleasant bars. In the bars you can buy plates of seafood, including whole crabs.

We toured the old town, the Alfama, on the outfit and had trouble fitting through some of the narrow, steep streets. There are excellent, cheap restaurants here, specialising once again in seafood, and we had marinated fried tuna and grilled sardines. The people gave us good-natured advice – don't park there, traffic comes around the corner so fast! There was so much gesticulating that I understood Portuguese quite easily.

Trams run through the alleyways, and on blind corners there are men with table tennis bats – one side red, the other green. When a tram comes along, they show you the red side of the bat and you stop. Portuguese policemen are rather more fortunate than the Spaniards and get BMWs on which to ride around. It was Millie's birthday, and we bought her a cake, which was much appreciated. We also found a laundromat and did some long-overdue washing, and I invested in a litre of the cheap and delicious local pear brandy.

It looks like a vandalised vehicle from Star Wars, but it's a Lisbon tram.

Going south again, we took the coast road through Simbales. It must have been a sleepy fishing village not too long ago, but has been caught up in the tourist trade now. A castle overlooks the town, looking suspiciously like a dozen other castles we'd seen in this country – I have a theory that they're mass-produced in cardboard and erected anywhere there are tourists, for atmosphere. Possibly they soak them in the kind of resin the East Germans were using for the Trabant cars, to make them rain-resistant.

Over lunch we were serenaded by a great flock of goats with bells around their necks. Shortly afterwards, I pulled out to overtake a truck and suddenly found a car coming the other way. I opened the throttle of the XS a little too far and we went past the truck on the back wheel. A rather unexpected bonus, considering the load we were carrying...

Our map showed a bridge across the river mouth here, but that turned out to be a misprint and we had to brave the Setubal one-way system again. Then we did something very naughty – an oil change by the side of the road, running the waste oil into a pit and covering it up. Considering that everyone else does the same thing, without covering it up, we didn't feel as guilty as we might have.

In the Sines campsite we watched the Magic Roundabout on TV, dubbed into Portuguese; it didn't seem to lose anything in the translation, and Zebedee was as cute as ever.

A German engineer we met suggested we take the mountain road rather than the coastal highway down to the Algarve. We were glad we'd followed his advice when we found a well surfaced, twisting road lined with enormous gum trees and pine forests. We did have one heart-stopper along here, however. I had just paid at a service station when I turned around and saw the Yamaha wreathed in smoke. By the time I was half-way to the sidecar for the fire extinguisher, I realised that it was just steam. The attendant had washed some spilt petrol off the tank and the water had vaporised on the hot engine. Quite a relief.

We had organised the catering so that one couple bought the food and cooked for a week and then handed over to the others. When Neil and Millie handed over to us down on the coast, they had overspent badly and we had another argument. The goodwill of Biarritz was wearing thin. Then Millie was cheated of £14 of the kitty, changing money at the border, and didn't notice until we'd crossed to Spain on the rickety old ferry. It wore even thinner. Regrettably, things that don't really seem to matter very much in normal life can take on great importance in the hothouse conditions of a long tour.

Our map showed a motorway from the border to Seville, but this turned out to exist only on paper, so we took longer to cover this stretch than anticipated. By the time we got onto the motorway to Cadiz, we were riding into the setting sun; and the last stage down to Algeciras was done in the dark. But it was a remarkably good road; we stopped for a roadside dinner with coffee and arrived at the campsite in good shape.

Neil and Millie took the XS to Granada to pick up the mail and Annie and I did some shopping for Africa, mostly packet soups and a bit of booze. We also chatted to a chopper-riding Swede in the campsite who had just returned from Morocco. He made it sound just like every other Muslim country I'd been to.

We were at the wharf quite early the next day to catch the ferry, and Annie went off to mail some letters while we were waiting. Neil and Millie decided to get the outfit on board to make sure it was out of harm's way, and disappeared down the dock. Then, ten minutes before time, our ferry cast off and sailed! Annie returned and we stood watching our companions disappearing around the mole. Or so we thought.

Just then, an elderly French chap I'd been talking with earlier came over and asked us if we weren't going to Ceuta. Of course we were, but – *regardez, la bateau marche.* "Oh, *non*," he said. The Ceuta boat was farther down the wharf, but we'd better get there *tout de suite* or it would go without us... Annie and I were on the bike, down the other end of the wharf and aboard the good ship *Virgin of Africa* in a time that would have made Graeme Crosby proud. I always did have a habit of jumping to conclusions.

CHAPTER 22

Morocco

"Morocco is the greatest. I should be getting money from the Moroccans because I'm just telling everyone that it's a wonderful place to go."
BILL MURRAY

GOING FROM SPAIN to Ceuta is pretty much just like crossing the English Channel; even the ferries are similar – the main differences are that you get a view of the Rock of Gibraltar on this one, the crossing only takes two hours and you stay in the same country. Ceuta is rather like a dusty, grubby Singapore with all the atmosphere of excitement that free ports get. The mailing slot in the post office is the mouth of an enormous brass lion's head, which impressed me no end. The story goes that if you tell a lie while your hand is in the lion's mouth, it will close and crush it. Not true. Heh.

The border was slow, but fairly relaxed. We were apprehensive, having heard horror stories, but the only horrible thing that happened was that we had to lay out a fortune for insurance. Customs seemed very keen on guns and radio transmitters, but we assured them the bikes held neither and they let us go.

We were stopped for papers twice before reaching our camp at Martil, but weren't delayed much. Over dinner we discussed the financial situation, for once without acrimony, and Annie took over the management of our funds from Millie. The Martil campground was quite reasonable, with a reassuring wall and trees. The amenities block, however, had a broken tank on the roof, which led to cascades of water pouring down the walls and over the door. It was rather like walking under a waterfall into a river cave to brush your teeth.

Tetouan, which we reached the next day, is the main tourist trap in the north and catches all the day-trippers from Spain. We parked in

Annie negotiates payment for fuel somewhere high in the Moroccan Atlas.

the main square while Annie went to change some money, and were handed all the usual lines: "I am from the tourist office. You are very fortunate, today there is the annual market, just one day..." We had been told about this line, and assured that the market was not only on every day of the year, it also had prices especially inflated for the suckers.

"You want some dope? My father grows best quality...." I get rid of these guys by quoting, with a straight face, a Reader's Digest story I once read on the horrors of "the weed". We had a bit of fun there in the square.

The road south through the Rif is lovely, with steep, scrubby hillsides reaching up to snowy peaks on both sides as it winds up to the plateau. After a stop to buy lunch at Chechaouen, a pretty little hill village, we pushed on towards Meknes - pushed on rather carefully, too, as the road was lined with some unpleasant car wrecks and we weren't keen to add a bike. The light was failing when we reached Meknes, and the politeness of a Moroccan bus driver nearly killed Annie and me. A lot of vehicles have a small green courtesy

We did not travel all the way to Morocco to be snowed in. So it goes.

light affixed to the back, which they flash when the road ahead is clear. I took this bloke's word – or rather light – for it, but he was wrong. I made it back into the line of traffic with inches to spare.

Meknes has a most attractive campsite, with lush grass, gum trees, flower beds and stands of banana plants, all surrounded by the walls of the old sultan's palace. The German girl with the 400/4 whom we'd met in France was here; she had teamed up with a chap on an XS750 which was currently a 500 twin. One cylinder stubbornly refused to fire. The army kept us awake that night with band and choir practice until the early hours. They were pretty good, though.

The Meknes medina, or old town, isn't particularly exciting, but there's a good, versatile bazaar and most of the fruit and vegetables had marked prices. After a while that comes as a relief, trust me. We indulged in a glass of the delicious mint tea that was to become our standard beverage in Morocco, and luckily didn't catch anything unpleasant from the grubby hole-in-the-wall tea house. Just after our return to camp it snowed. The guards were delighted and told us that this was their first snow for 15 years. A lot of good that was to us, camped out in it! We'd had enough of the cold, and headed for the coast and then south.

Rabat was a very European and not particularly interesting sort of city, and at Casablanca we struck the only bit of motorway in the country. Everyone really liked it – you could see that by the traffic, which consisted of everything from pedestrians through buggies to loaded camels, ambling every which way. There was very little motorised traffic, which was just as well as it would probably have disturbed the people living under the bridges.

After a night in a nasty campsite at Mohammedia, which seemed to be inhabited solely by rapacious cats – one slept in my helmet and one chewed its way into most of our dried soups – we pushed on to Essaouira. As we were rolling south through the rather dull countryside, I plotted a way in which I could attend my own wake. I would organise it when I got back to Australia . . . amazing what idle minds will turn to. The campground was pleasant and run by a bloke who looked like an ASIO (Australian Security and Intelligence Organisation) spook in his shades and jungle jacket.

Farther south it became noticeably drier, and the goats had to climb trees to get at edible bits of greenery. We stopped to photograph some of them and became embroiled in an elaborate arrangement as to how much to pay which of the herd boys who clustered around for the right to take photos of the goats. "Whose goats are those?" – "Yes, yes!" – "No, whose goats are those?" – "Yes, one dirham, yes!"

There is an abrupt rocky drop to sea level along this road that reminded me of Eucla on the Nullarbor Plain. We stopped to chat with a group of surfies, who reported some tent slashing and stealing in their impromptu beach camp, but who were much more interested in how the swell was farther north. Disappointing, we told them. Flat.

We stayed at the tourist campsite in Agadir, mostly because it had hot showers, and spent Christmas Day sitting around the pool, drinking beer and wondering what the poor people were doing. Agadir is a tourist resort like any other, with the same hotels and conducted tours, and didn't hold much for us. Except those hot showers.

Fresh sardines, straight off the boat and grilled in front of you in Essaouira. Ahh!

We went south to the edge of the desert at Tiznit and then out along the dirt road "*piste*" to Sidi Moussa. Along this stretch there was a bridge with a prominent "detour" sign pointing down into the sandy river bed. Being good law-abiding citizens, we toiled through the deep sand with the bikes only to see a loaded truck go past on the bridge. Such is life. Sidi Moussa turned out to be a grimy, derelict place with one campsite covered in rocks and another deep in sand, all inhabited by dubious-looking Europeans drawing on funny cigarettes.

As the war had closed all the roads, we could go no farther south, so it was unanimously decided to go back and spend some time in Essaouira. On the way, we were pulled over by police, who just wanted to have a look at the bikes. One of them allowed that he wouldn't mind an XS 1100 himself, but his BMW was so simple to repair that it was more sensible in Morocco. His friend looked familiar, and I soon realised that he could have been a rather slimmer Idi Amin. Lo! How the mighty are fallen....

Rolling into the Essaouira campsite, we were just behind another Australian couple, Michel and Cathy Mol, aboard a BMW R100S.

Our camp in Essaouira was nearly perfect, except there was no hot water.

They camped with us and we all employed ourselves lazing about in the sun. They joined us for the New Year's Eve fire on the beach, too, and Cathy absorbed a little too much of the local rough red wine. Being a gentleman, I won't go into details, but Michel had his hands full for a while. We had had to ride all the way down to Agadir to buy the wine, so it was a bit of a waste really...

Time passed quickly, as it often does when you're doing nothing, and we spent a lot of time just wandering around the harbour and fortifications of the town, which had once been a Portuguese trading post and had the cannons to prove it. The gates to the medina were still defended by bulky bronze mortars, now serving as never-emptied rubbish bins. Freshly grilled sardines, straight from the boats, were an attraction on the wharf. One group of campers was permanently stoned, and it took them four hours to collect their meagre belongings when they left. They then wandered vaguely off in different directions. I guess they got a lift, because we didn't see them again.

The campsite, "defended" by seven dogs augmented by four pups, became a home from home to us. One evening, a little fat-tyred 125 Suzuki fun bike rolled in. The occupants eyed the XS 1100, R100S and GS 750 outfit parked near our tents and the female pillion, whose motorcycle clothing was a ragged-looking fur coat, asked diffidently, "Do any of you know anything about motorbikes?" We allowed that we might, just a little, and asked what was wrong.

It turned out that the tiny bike would only rev out to twenty-two hundred, and then died. My first suspicion was the sparkplug, because I'd had similar problems with my XL. But it wasn't that, as we found out when we unbolted the carburettor float bowl. This was filled with what looked like fat white worms. The rider then remembered that he'd had a petrol leak from the lip of the bowl, and put sealing compound on it and bolted it back in place. He must have used a whole tube, because the stuff had squeezed out and set in the bowl, forming the worms and stopping the float from moving. The bike had been like this for a thousand miles, they told us.

I hope they made it home to Switzerland.

Annie does the food shopping in Essaouira in one of the friendly market stalls.

Annie got an abscess on a tooth and had to go to the local dentist. Although she claimed afterwards that he had been quite good, her heartrending screams under treatment suggested differently. The chap was so concerned about hurting her that he waived most of his fee. There's a tip there...

The Yamaha's battery ran flat, too. Mind you, we had been tapping it for our fluorescent camping light for a couple of weeks without running the engine – not entirely recommended. I was grateful for the accessory kickstarter, because push starting didn't work and this way we could run some improvised jump leads from the BMW while I kicked – the leads wouldn't carry enough current by themselves to use the electric starter. They nearly melted as it was.

The fine weather broke towards the middle of January and we moved on to Marrakesh and more blue skies. The Mols came with us, and it felt like a bike club run with the three machines. Camp was made in the larger and cheaper of the two rocky Marrakesh sites and although hygiene left something to be desired, it was a relaxed sort of place and we settled in well.

Marrakesh was like something out of the Thousand and One Nights. The old main square, the Djemaa El Fna, was filled with conjurers, fire-eaters, snake charmers, dentists, acrobats, musicians and traders at all hours of the day. The intricate passageways of the souks, the markets, held fascinating workshops and good bargains – if you haggled carefully. We left the bikes outside in the care of the human parking meters, attendants with large brass plaques which they wore proudly and ostentatiously. You had to bargain with them, too, over the parking fees, but they were conscientious.

Our most spectacular coup came in the campsite. An old bloke was selling warm, fuzzy, striped blankets, and he had one that was really lovely. His starting price was 350 dirhams, and he assured us that this was not his "rich tourist price". After an entire evening of dedicated haggling, he settled for 35 dirhams, a t-shirt, two pairs of socks, a shirt, a tie (no, I don't know either) and . . . one of Annie's bras. He had a little trouble figuring out what this wispy nylon thing was, but he got the idea when we held it onto his chest. Then he was

The campsite at Fez was a welcome opportunity to just relax.

hugely amused. "*Ah, pour madame!*" he beamed.

In town, we found warm showers, in a *hamam* (bathhouse) next to the Regent Cinema. The first warm showers for a month, and you could stay under them for as long as you liked. Ah, luxury.

The Mols, Annie and I spent one evening on a cafe balcony overlooking the Djeema el Fna, watching the trading and performing going on below us by the light of pressure lanterns. When we got back to the bikes, we were overwhelmed by a crowd of little boys, perhaps five years old on average, who, like a locust swarm, proceeded to pick our pockets and climb all over us and the bikes. They disappeared like smoke when a soldier came along. It was just as well that he came by, for how do you defend yourself against five-year-olds?

Annie and I took the Yamaha up to the snowy pass leading inland over the Atlas, to see if it was possible to get across to Ourzazate. The road was mostly clear, and where there was snow or ice on the surface the truck drivers had been spreading gravel. So the caravan of bikes moved on over Tichka Pass and down into the western margins of the Sahara. The Atlas is quite lovely here, with sheer rock flanks and

If you're at all interested in crystals, I have just the place for you.

tiny stone villages, all shrouded in snow. We stopped in Taddert for tea and were bombarded with demands that we buy handfuls of the sparkling crystals found around there, but we managed to resist the temptation. Just over the pass there was a bus lying by the side of the road. It had taken a corner too wide and rolled three times. Although the casualties had been taken away, we could still see the rust-brown stains of blood on the broken window glass, a chilling reminder to ride carefully.

Ourzazate boasted a basic but comfortable campsite – it had running water and a helpful caretaker-cum-guard, who looked after us to the extent of making a fire of palm fronds in a tin and preparing tea for everyone on it. There was also a good market and a much-detested Club Mediterranee. The local people all resented the place because it bought nothing from them.

We pushed on north along the flanks of the Atlas, over narrow and often broken desert roads. This felt like the real desert, with very little vegetation and occasional small herds of camels or goats. At El Kelaa an old man in a torn djellaba came up to us and started extolling the virtues of sidecars in a mixture of French, German and Arabic (or maybe Berber; it was hard to tell). He had fought in the Second World War on the side of the Germans and they, he told us, had had sidecars with machine guns on them! And the British had come over in aeroplanes, shooting, and the French had shot him in this leg right here. Oh dear, what a lot of fun the war had been . . . he sounded just like some of the old soldiers back home.

The Ksar es Souk campsite had deep grass and trees but very little water. We had also run out of gas for our stove and small bottles were unobtainable, so we ate sandwiches. Later, someone told us that there was a spring just outside town where there was plenty of water and free camping, as well as palm leaves to make a fire. Ah, well.

On the way back up into the mountains we had almost alpine scenery up to the Col du Zad where we had a snowball fight. After that it looked more like the end of the world. A high plateau, bare and windswept, with snowdrifts huddling against black rock piles,

Wherever we went, it was the Suzuki with the sidecar that drew most attention.

this was one of the grimmest places I'd ever seen after the Anatolian Highlands. It went on for quite a few miles, the road snow-ploughed clear to one car's width, and we felt the cold creeping in even under our excellent Britax Alaskan suits. The plateau ended very abruptly and the road dropped through pine forests to the red tile roofs of the very French resort town of Ifrane.

A few miles later, over good roads, we were in Fes, the new part of which looked very French too. The old town was straight out of the Dark Ages, with its narrow, convoluted, noisy passageways. We actually employed a guide – the first time I'd ever done that – and it was just as well, even though he was more interested in taking us to his friend's shops than showing us the town. We would never have found our way out alone. The next day was my birthday, and I was presented with a cake. Then sixteen buses loaded with 600 Danish schoolchildren invaded the camp. They came in the morning and left in the evening without ever looking at the town. A mystery.

We took advantage of the ridiculously low postage charges to send our souvenirs home and had the parcel wrapped very professionally by the semi-official parcel wrapper at the post office. He had a folder full of letters of appreciation from past customers, which he insisted we peruse while he wrapped.

After arranging to meet us again in Athens, the Mols took their leave to return to England and we turned towards the Algerian border. After an oil and filter change by the side of the road we rode past Taza, pretty on its hilltop, up to a famous cave in the mountains. The steps leading down were in woeful condition and when, months later in London, I saw a photo I'd taken of it, it revealed *"Bon courage"* scribbled on the wall near the bottom. It had been too dark to see this cheerful note while we were down there. We camped in the showground at Taza, watched by a cute and inquisitive donkey which then tried to steal our food and threatened to bite when we tried to chase it off.

There was no problem about obtaining Algerian visas at Oujda, near the border, except that we had arrived on one of the innumerable Muslim holidays. So it was off to the border and the only campsite, to wait for three days and, in the cafe, watch the worst TV programs we'd ever been subjected to. Egyptian soap operas seem to have the lowest budgets, for sets anyway, of any shows I've ever seen. Every time someone closed a door the walls shook.

I had a nasty bout of 'flu, and lay in the tent drugged to the eyeballs while tempers again deteriorated around me. I didn't help by snapping at anyone who came near me. In the end I got fed up with it all and suggested we split up as soon as we were out of the desert.

When the consulate finally reopened, one of the questions on the visa application form was, "Will you be sufficient during your stay in Algeria?" The bloke opposite me, filling out his own form, grinned and said, "I guess the only answer to that is 'Quite'," so that's what we both put down. Insurance was much cheaper than it had been at the Moroccan border and we were processed quite quickly.

Algeria

THEN THE "*route rapide*" of the map turned out to be the "*road lente*", because it was less than half finished and we got to Tlemcen tired and dirty. It took ages to find the campground; none of the locals seemed to know it existed, but when we did find it, it was comfortable and free – the only real drawback was a watchdog that delighted in untying people's shoelaces and chewing through tent ropes.

I collapsed again as soon as the tents were up, still feeling ill, and things started getting heated again. Neil insisted that we split up right there and then. He was right, too – if it isn't working, don't drag out the agony. We slept on it, and I think he was a little surprised when I started sorting out the gear in the morning. We divided the equipment and Annie and I, on a rather overloaded Yamaha, set off down into the Sahara. By ourselves.

Feeling very much at peace with the world we buzzed across northern Algeria, with a short stop for coffee, and on into the greening countryside. Spring was in the air, people waved to us and we swept around the tolerably well-surfaced twisting roads in a thoroughly good mood.

> "*I'm Algerian.
> We don't keep calm.*"
> T-SHIRT

Then half the gear we had balanced precariously on the back of the bike fell off – we lost our spare visors, Annie's shoes and some food, but we weren't particularly perturbed. Even the obstinacy of the police in Tiaret and Songeur didn't bother us much. The tourist office had assured us that these worthies would point out places to camp where there were no official sites, but all they would do was direct us to a hotel. "You are rich Europeans, you can afford it." Pleas of antipodean motorcycling poverty fell on deaf ears.

But it was all for the best. A farmer just outside Songeur was considerably more helpful; not only was he glad to offer us a place to

The signposting in the Sahara is good, distances are reminiscent of Australia.

With the wonderfully hospitable family on the farm at Songeur. Thanks again!

pitch our tent, but he supplied us with milk and eggs and refused to take any payment. The whole family cheered us as we rode away in the morning. Algeria was turning out to be a much more hospitable place than it had been painted in Morocco.

It was getting noticeably drier now, and as we neared Laghouat we entered the desert proper. Vegetation, which had been scarce for a hundred miles or so, disappeared completely and so did the few flocks of goats and sheep; only the camels remained. Shops became scarce, too, in the few towns we saw and we found it difficult to buy bread. On this day Annie finally got some in a restaurant in Laghouat.

The Saharan roads weren't bad, but roadworks meant frequent detours through deep sand which were rather trying. The bike handled them well considering it was now loaded up with all our camping gear, food reserves and 30 litres of fuel and water, but the sand was still a strain. We were glad to see Ghardaia, our first real oasis, and its jolly but expensive campsite. We even popped up to the Big Hotel and had a drink. Considering how much wine Algeria produces it is damn hard to get any in the country itself.

One French traveler had a copy of the Fabulous Michelin 135 - the map of the Sahara crossing that's been out of print and totally unobtainable for years - so I borrowed it and made a few notes in my diary; then it was on to El Golea. The desert scenery, which was flat, without hills or dunes, and with rock-covered sand to the horizon was rapidly becoming boring. The one bit of relief on this leg was an enormous golfball on an even more enormous tee just before El Golea - it turned into a microwave repeater when we got close.

There was more flatness the next day on the way down to Ain Salah. I was a bit worried about the road surface before lunch, but a meal made all the difference and I relaxed in the afternoon. Food is an excellent medicine for the jitters.

The truckies down in the desert were painfully polite, and would pull off the narrow tar when they saw us coming. The only problem was that once on the dirt they would then throw up an impenetrable screen of dust, which hid the road, so you never knew if there was another truck behind the first. If there had been we would have been decorating his radiator.

"Where did you get the flat motorbike motif, Abdul?" "It just came to me one day...."

The bike returned nearly 49mpg (imp) on this leg, the best it did on the entire trip, which was a testament to the flatness of the Sahara. Short of hills it might have been but the road was bumpy with shallow potholes, no more than an inch deep, which I learnt to ignore.

Ain Salah was a strange town; built of mud, or concrete covered with mud, it sat in the desert like a low rock outcrop. Where did they get the water to make mud? Aside from a half dozen lackadaisical cafes, it seemed to lack shops, even the markets selling only oranges and carrots. Despite its isolation - it must be just about in the exact middle of the desert - Ain Salah is a cosmopolitan place; I guess they get all types coming through. We were warned not to camp in the "palmeries", the palm plantations, because of the mosquitoes. They got us anyway, despite the fact that we sought out a little stand of palms way out in the middle of the sands; Annie returned to the tent badly stung after answering the call of nature.

We held a council of war the next morning and decided that enough Sahara as enough. There is only one road down through the desert and you must return the way you came. That would have meant looking at the same flat nothingness for an extra three or four days, and we decided we'd rather spend the time somewhere more exciting.

Then we tried to ride out to the road. The back wheel of the Yamaha simply dropped through the crust of sand and spun uselessly. We unpacked the bike, removing everything we could including the panniers, and then Annie pushed while I revved the bike as hard as I could. Slowly it began to move, and then it almost jumped back up onto the crust and I rode like blazes for the sealed roadway.

On the way back the little palm-lined campsite in El Golea sheltered us for a while, and we explored this huge oasis and its surroundings – Annie even tried out the bathhouse, but wasn't impressed. One afternoon, a Land-Rover with two Australian women aboard rolled up. One of them got out and said, "Geez, I'd give my soul for a cold

Camping, not by the palmeries at Ain Salah, but found by mosquitoes anyway.

beer." We directed them to the one "good" hotel in town which had stocks of this foreign substance.

Our return to Ghardaia was uneventful – more sand and rocks – and we had a look around this "second Mecca", so called because parts of the valley are still closed to non-Muslims. Then we set off for El Oued and the Tunisian border, and rode straight into the teeth of a sandstorm. By the time we had turned east it had become a crosswind and was throwing the fully laden bike all over the road – on one memorable occasion, even into the deep roadside sand. Coupled with the limited visibility of about 20 feet it was too much for me and we turned around.

The most excruciatingly boring day followed as we sat in the tent and listened to the wind howling outside. After the third game of Scrabble and a couple of Mastermind we just sat there and stared at the canvas. But it had settled down the next morning and we made good time across – you guessed it – more flat desert. But near El Oued the country changed and soon we were riding through, and sometimes over, enormous sand dunes. This was the Great Western Erg, the sandy desert you see in the movies. By the side of the road, the telegraph wires often disappeared into the tops of dunes, only to reappear on the other side. Communications must be dire. We also saw date palms and herds of camels, and decided that this was much more like it. Why couldn't the whole Sahara look like this?

CHAPTER 24

Tunisia

"Tunisia is always ready to turn the page."
HABIB BOURGUIBA

EXCEPT WHEN STAMPING your passport, it seemed. When we reached Hazoua, the Tunisian border post, a slight problem emerged. The tourist bureau leaflet had assured us that visas were issued at the border, but the sergeant on guard thought otherwise. "Not possible."

I told him about the leaflet and he smiled gently and said, "Ah, the tourist bureau, it is their job to get people to come to my country but it is my job to keep them out." Problem. We couldn't go back, as our single-visit Algerian visas had been cancelled half an hour earlier at the Algerian border, and we couldn't go forward because this officious idiot wouldn't let us. We couldn't really stay there, either. Without money changing facilities or a shop for even the most basic necessities, Hazoua didn't really make it as a campsite.

But one of the skills you develop if you travel a lot is knowing when to shout and when to whisper and I decided this was a shouting situation. So I waved my press card and introductory letter at the sergeant. The letter, from *Middle East Travel Magazine* where I had been art director, was in Arabic and impressed the guard sufficiently for him to get on the radio. He came back and said, perhaps, but it would take three days. We sat down to wait. I was fairly confident they wouldn't let us starve, and I was right.

One of the guards saw me rubbing Nivea (another sponsor, thank you!) into my hands and delightedly shouted "You are woman! You are woman!" I invited him to look at the monster that our XS11 Yamaha had become with all of its fairings and our luggage. "Could you ride that? No? Then beware whom you insult." He gave us half his dinner, and some of the others kicked in as well.

Then followed a hectic night for all. The guards were nervous and afraid of the Lybians, who had attacked the nearby town of Gafsa a few days earlier, and they spent the night prowling around with loaded guns and flashlights. We slept first on the veranda and then, at the guards' invitation in the Customs post, more afraid of those guns than of the Lybians. A false alarm involving a Belgian camper van which had scared the sentries lightened the atmosphere a little as the terrified Belgians were dragged in at gunpoint and interrogated.

"Do you think we are fools? What were you doing out there? I do not care if you are a policeman!" North African French is relatively easy to understand because it has a small vocabulary and no grammar whatsoever, so we could follow all this. It was nevertheless confusing; why pick on these people? One of the guards came out and winked at us. "Belgians!" he grinned.

Things looked better in the morning. The Chef du Poste (who is the boss, not the cook) arrived and cut through some of the red

Refueling the bike with a repurposed Duckham's (another sponsor, thank you) oil canister.

tape, and with visas in our passports there finally seemed to be a way forward. But we needed duty stamps for the visas, and they were obtainable only in the next town.

"We shall do this," said the Chef du Poste. "You," pointing at me, "will take the motorcycle to get the stamps. She," pointing at Annie, "will remain here."

"Ah, no."

"Then we shall do this. You and she and this guard will go on the motorcycle to get the stamps."

"Ah... no. Why don't we just ride to the town and get the stamps? Of course we will return."

"Ah, no. We shall do this. The guard with your passports will take the bus. You two will follow on the motorcycle. You will pay for the stamps and the guard will give you back the passports."

"Ah, yes. Thank you."

"No, no, it is nothing... welcome to Tunisia." All of this in the broken North African French, of course, mine considerably more broken than his.

There was one more hurdle, however, in the form of a police checkpoint just outside town. The bus was checked and went on. Then it was our turn. As I tried to explain in my combination of schoolboy and gutter French that the passports the cop wanted to see were on the bus (*voila, les passports, er, marchons dans le autobus!*), he became more and more annoyed and began to toy with his sidearm. Fortunately, the guard on the bus remembered us round about then and made the bus turn back. He was abused for inefficiency by the cop, who then let us pass with a big, toothy grin.

Tunisia didn't really turn out to be worth all the trouble. We rode up to the coast at Nabeul through uninspiring country, camped and went into Tunis to pick up mail and book the ferry to Sicily. Annie scouted out a replacement gas bottle for our stove, which was a relief. Nice to be able to do your own cooking.

We moved to a hotel in Tunis for our last night, because the ferry left at 6.30 am and the nearest campsite was two hours from the port.

The Hotel Medina was nice; our hosts insisted that we park in the lobby, which I'd intended to do anyway. Then we went out and bought some English newspapers as well as pate, salami and bread, and had a feast of eating and reading in our room. We explored the medina as well and found it pretty if a little tame, discovered the excellent produce markets and then slept until one am. Then the alarm on Annie's little calculator, the desk clerk and the muezzin from the nearby mosque woke us simultaneously.

Getting the bike into the hotel lobby had been easy with a dozen helping hands, but now that it was just Annie, the desk clerk and me it wasn't quite so easy to get it out. After a 36-point turn, scuffing their paintwork with my front tyre on every one, I managed it and we rode off down to the ferry followed by the desk clerk's blessings.

While we were waiting aboard the big Yamaha in the light, sprinkling rain for them to open the gates, an XS500 arrived ... then an XL125 ... then two bicycles. I kept expecting someone on a skateboard. After an elaborate check of papers, which failed to turn up the fact that we had overstayed our visas, and a confused Customs check, we finally rolled aboard. Back to Europe!

CHAPTER 25

Italy

> *"As they say in Italy, Italians were eating with a knife and fork when the French were still eating each other."*
> MARIO BATALI

THE FERRY TO Trapani wasn't exactly the QE2, but it got us there; everything was rather shabby and the bar and restaurant were expensive and generally closed. In the third class saloon, where we made our home for the 12 hours of the crossing, there was strict segregation – the Arabs sat on one side, we Europeans on the other. The curious thing was that you didn't actually see this division happen – it just developed. When we first sat down, there was an Arab family sitting near us, then, as more Europeans arrived and sat on our side, they moved.

We spent most of the crossing playing cards with the French guys riding the bikes we'd met at the gate. True to form, these two let me struggle along in my idiot French until they wanted to explain something about the game we were playing – and then they both suddenly spoke passable English. The French are hilarious; they always do that sort of thing.

The Immigration check in Sicily must have been carefully designed for the absolute minimum in efficiency, but the Customs check that followed was considerably keener – it involved our first encounter with drug-sniffing dogs. One of them, a cheerful hyperactive German Shepherd, was much more interested in chewing our tentpoles than in looking for drugs. I politely asked the handler to restrain his beast.

Then it was out into the chilly, wet evening and up the autostrada to Palermo. Sicily in the failing light was almost unbearably picturesque, although I'm sure I would have enjoyed it more had I been warm and

Gibellina in Sicily had an earthquake in 1968. It's still a bit rough.

dry. We reached the "Pepsi Cola" campsite just as it was closing, and the *padrone* took us into the office and poured us a brandy before we got down to the signing-in formalities. Sicilians are very perceptive people.

It dawned wet and cold, so we inserted ourselves into our Alaskan suits and MCB boots – waterproof boots are a real blessing when you get several days of rain – and went exploring. The site watchman warned us to beware of pickpockets in Palermo, but apart from the post office giving us change in stamps rather than cash we weren't robbed.

Northern Sicily is a rugged place, with awe-inspiring cliffs sheltering long ranges of hills like overstuffed pillows, with a fine needlework of vineyards embroidered on them. Despite the drizzle, we had an enjoyable few days exploring. Every now and then the *padrone* back at camp would get worried about us and offer us alternative accommodation – first it was a little wooden house, then a caravan. All free of charge. He couldn't understand that we were quite happy in our tent.

As the skies looked clearer to the south, we finally packed, had a last cup of coffee in our little bar on the harbour and headed across the island to Selinunte. We rode through seemingly endless fields of yellow flowers and discovered a peculiar system of motorways. These roads weren't on our map, and seemed almost like miniatures – a proper motorway scaled down to Fiat 500 size. Altogether in poor repair, the system didn't seem to lead anywhere. I had some vague memory of the fascists undertaking construction programs in economically depressed parts of Sicily; this could well have been one of them.

A chap we met along the way showed us a rather eerie place to have our picnic lunch – the main square of Gibellina, a town destroyed by an earthquake in 1968 and never rebuilt. We were stopped by the police a little later, but our total inability to speak Italian foiled them and they let us go. I've found that ignorance is generally bliss when talking to cops.

Sometimes the sights in Italy like this temple are actually Greek.

The Greek temple at Selinunte was in better condition than most of the ones in Greece itself, but the campsite that had been recommended to us there didn't seem to exist. We carried on to camp at Sciacca, after endless rows of holiday houses in various stages of incompletion and invariable poor taste. The sun came out, and in the morning we were served excellent Espresso coffee right at our tent. A great institution, the waiter-service campsite.

As Caltanisetta's bypass road wasn't quite finished, we had to go through the town itself. This is the one environment in which a heavily loaded XS1100 really doesn't shine. The narrow, cobbled streets with their sharp corners gave me quite a bit to do. An additional problem is that you can't get yourself out of trouble with the throttle – there's nowhere for the bike to go if you accelerate. We were caught in a Communist Party march as well, which slowed us down even more. Caltanisetta had good ice-cream, though.

Down past Enna, we took the spectacular autostrada, which just ignores the lie of the land. When it isn't swinging itself over the valleys on a "*viadotto*" it's drilling through the hills in a tunnel. It must have cost an absolute fortune to build.

On the coast once again, this time the eastern one, we found a supposedly closed campground called "Bahia del Silenzio" at Brucoli, which opened just for us. With typical kindness, the people offered us a small bungalow, but we stuck with the old tent. We'd finally woken up to the most economical way to supply ourselves with wine, and bought a five litre plastic container which we regularly refilled with the local vintage just like the Italians do.

After a quick look at Neapolis with its amphitheatre, near Syracuse, we turned north once more, to Catania. The inland road looked good on the map and turned out to be quite exciting, with steep hills and ridgetop runs, but on the way back down it became a little too exciting when we hit a sizeable patch of diesel and went sideways for a little while. No damage, but a bit of heavy breathing and cursing resulted.

A very thorough tour of Catania then, helped by the motorway signs, which pointed around in a large circle taking in most of the town. We both got really annoyed with this and rode around swearing at the tops of our voices until at last the autostrada entry ramp came into view. Fortunately, the Italian motorway cafes serve excellent coffee. We recovered our composure over cappuccino.

Camp was at Acireale, just north of Catania, in a clifftop campsite that had a lift running down to the beach. Talk about luxury. Another sort-out left us with quite a bit of gear to mail home, and we parceled it all up neatly and took it up to the post office. It wasn't to be that simple, though. First of all, I hadn't left enough loose string for them to put their metal seal on. They retied the parcel for me. Then, I hadn't put a return address on it. I tried to tell them that I certainly didn't want the parcel returned to the campsite, but it seemed that a return address was required by law. So I put the same address on the parcel twice, which made them very unhappy, but they took it. Losing a little weight made the bike look much neater.

We rode up around Mount Etna, through hazelnut plantations and past pretty little towns balanced on hilltops, and on north through a national park and a vast hunting reserve. Lovely country up here, with some excellent road over the passes that took us to Milazzo and a German-run campsite called, inexplicably, "sayonara". The weather was pleasant but the locals still seemed to find it wintry. At a petrol stop on the way to Messina, the attendant came out of his office shaking his head, pointing to the bike and crying "Freddo! Freddo!", which I took to mean "cold" in Italian. Either that or he'd mistaken the bike for a friend of his called Fred; unlikely under the circumstances.

The ferry to San Giovanni on the toe of Italy was quick and cheap. They once again had excellent coffee on the ferry, and nice pastries, but the signposting out of San Giovanni reminded us unpleasantly of Catania. When we finally made it out of town, we rode up the coast through Scylla (Charybdis must have given up monstering, it wasn't to be seen) and on north. People seemed rather offhand and not particularly friendly, even suspicious. When we tried to change some money at an airport, the teller regretted that the bank had run out of money. Fruit and vegetables didn't seem as fresh as those in Sicily, and the roads were worse.

We really didn't think much of southern Italy. There was a lovely campsite in an olive grove at Lamezia Terme, admittedly. We took to the autostrada to get us north – it's free as far as Salerno as some kind of odd economic boost for the south – and we followed it up through the southern mountains, past occasional snow patches, with our warm clothes, heated handlebar grips and GloGloves on. The hills were lovely, with only a few factories polluting the air.

Naples welcomed us with its expensive but invaluable "tangentiale" ring road, which introduced us to a new and, as far as I know, unique hazard. I was used to buzzing up between stationary lanes of traffic, such as the ones queuing to pay toll on the ring road. Even with the rather wide Yamaha that had always worked. Not in Naples. None of the tiny Fiats I was trying to pass had air conditioning, so when they stopped in the queue they would throw open their doors. Oops! We weren't going to get through that! We nevertheless followed the ring road to its western end in Pozzuoli and a campground that had been highly praised. The site featured a swimming pool fed by a hot spring, and we spent as much time in the water as possible. Pozzuoli is famous for two things: it is the most earthquake-prone place in Italy, and it is the birthplace of Sophia Loren. We did feel some "trembles" but Sophia didn't seem to be home. I met her many years later at an Italian motorcycle industry dinner. She must have been in her mid-80s, and she looked stunning. Where was I?

Ah yes. Naples itself was a disappointment. It seemed to be little more than a permanent traffic jam; we were glad to get out. Pompeii was the real attraction and we spent some satisfying hours there. With a little imagination, the town comes alive just as it was before the ashes of Vesuvius swallowed it.

Annie and I also looked through the creepy underground ruins at Cumae, with their huge trapezoidal tunnels. On a lighter note, we bought a little chess set and I discovered to my delight that I could actually beat Annie. Only because she hadn't played before ... Neil and Millie were there, too, both looking well. They'd had a little

Rome is a great motorcycle city. You can essentially do what you like.

trouble with the GS in the desert when one of the carburetors had jammed and drained the petrol tank in less than 40 miles, without their noticing. The locals had helped them.

We rode up to Rome in bright sunshine by way of Cassino and the Via Appia, picked up our mail and found the "Roma" campsite without any trouble. Along the way, we discovered that the intricate Rome one way system doesn't apply to bikes. You can ride anywhere you like, in any direction. At one point we scattered the crowds around the Trevi fountain.

There were lots of fellow Australasians at the camp, and we spent most evenings standing around the fire drinking beer and telling lies. Because we'd taken the bike off to be serviced, we had to use public transport for getting around. This consisted mostly of buses like enormous green tin sheds on wheels, which are free. Well, they do have a ticket machine, but the only people who seemed to use it were the nuns. Nobody ever appeared to check for tickets. We visited the Colosseum and the Capitoline Hill, which was inhabited by a great tribe of tough looking cats. They are protected by law, it seems, and fed by the inevitable little old ladies. The catacombs were closed, allegedly for renovation. Renovating the sewers, how nice.

For us, the highlight was the Vatican Museum. Not so much for the Sistine Chapel, which looks and feels like an ecclesiastical railway station with a nice ceiling, but for the superb ethnological section.

With the bike back on the road, though not greatly improved by Italian servicing, we took in the more remote spots like the Villa d'Este, with its hundreds of fountains, and Hadrian's villa. One night, the Goodyear blimp put on a brilliant lightshow over the city. While we sat on a park bench craning our necks, moving coloured pictures flitted across the sky – we were entranced.

Before departing for Umbria we bought some new clothes, which was a real luxury after living in the same very limited range of clothing for so long. Our first stop was Assisi, with its houses of honey-coloured stone stacked one on top of the other on the hillside and a quiet campsite overlooking it all. The tomb of St Francis, deep in the rock, was very impressive. We had some pleasant sunshine, but it was still cold in the shade – as I discovered when I washed my one and only jacket.

It was wet and windy again on the road to Florence and we were forced to fortify ourselves frequently with coffee and cakes. Having arrived, we decided to cop out for once and stay in a pension. We were sick of the rain and wanted to feel warm, clean and human for a change. Punishment came, of course – someone broke into the bike's top box and stole the only thing in it, our airbed pump. I had locked the steering, put the alarm and the massive Abus lock on as well as covering the bike with the Vetter cover, but all to no avail. I guess we didn't do too badly, all things considered. The pump was the only thing stolen on the entire trip.

Our pension was comfortable, with en-suite bathroom featuring a working hot shower and central heating. A little time was spent outside – we looked at the Ponte Vecchio, wandered the streets drooling at the shop windows and toured the Uffizi gallery. I become very easily overloaded when confronted with too much art in one

The snow was deep across the mountains, but the road had been cleared effectively.

stroke, and emerged shell shocked. Annie coped much better.

Then it was back out into the rain and off to the mountains and the snow, but the road over to the east coast had been freshly cleared; it was empty of traffic and fun on the bike. We rode up the mountain to San Marino with the big motor enjoying the work. Hills were never a problem for the Yamaha and I very rarely even had to change down.

San Marino was a real, genuine tourist trap of the first order; a gem of a rip-off. The only good value was booze, so we stocked up. It was cold, too, and we huddled in our sleeping bag waiting for the morning, which brought a dullish run to Venice, where we installed ourselves in the Treviso campsite across the lagoon.

Venice repays the effort made to get away from the main tourist haunts; there's a wealth of interest in the back streets and alleys, and coffee is cheaper, too. Perhaps the place is a little too devoted to chasing the lire, but it's nonetheless interesting for all that. All the dogs wear muzzles, by the way, although some of them have their pacifiers just slung casually around their necks without interfering with the use of the teeth at all. Very Italian.

I felt inspired that night – perhaps Venice had kindled a fire in my soul – and excelled myself at dinner, even if I do say so myself. With only two pots and one flame I produced hamburgers, mashed potatoes with onions and mushrooms in white sauce. Didn't taste too bad either...

CHAPTER 26

Yugoslavia

*"At night, you can't do anything,
because all of Belgrade is lit by a ten-watt bulb,
and you can't go anywhere, because
Tito has the car..."*

MEL BROOKS

ITALY HAD SEEMED tame to us after the rigors of North Africa, so we were rather looking forward to Yugoslavia. We didn't have long to wait before things got rigorous again. At the border, the official took one look at our pretty blue Australian passports, went into a huddle with his pals and then disappeared indoors. Here he got on the telephone, looking worried and leaving us sitting in the drizzle without an explanation. All I could think of was that there had been some reports of terrorist training camps for an anti-government right-wing organisation called Ustashi in Australia. Perhaps the border police thought we were Ustashi shock troops, on a Yamaha. Eventually they decided to take a chance that we wouldn't blow up any bridges and let us in.

On to Zagreb with a will, through pretty, agricultural country with the first flush of spring on it and the last clouds of winter above it, but one of Zagreb's alleged campsites had disappeared. The other was closed, and so were most of the cheap hotels. We checked into a reasonably comfortable place near the railway station and went out to do the town, but the grim weather made that a rather uncomfortable pursuit, so we retired early and wrote letters.

We had intended to devote a day to the famous Plitvice lakes south of Zagreb. The rain became heavier and colder as we rode out of town, and the bike began to run rough and lose power. I pulled into a petrol station in Slunj – what a name for a town to get stuck with, although it is very pretty – and took parts of the fairing off. The problem wasn't difficult to trace. One of the plug leads had come undone and been casually pushed back, which I can only presume had happened during the service in Rome. It was soon fixed and gave no more trouble, which is more than I can say for the Yugoslav weather.

When we got to the lakes the rain turned to sleet, so we decided to get the hell out of there and down to the coast. Then, naturally, I got lost. The bloke behind the counter of a hardware/booze shop gave us directions. It seemed like an odd range of stock for a shop, but the more I thought about it, the more sense it made.

"I'll take a hammer and a box of tacks. Oh, and give me a flask of brandy. Two."

Back on the main road I overtook a truck without realising that there was a dip in the road ahead; the dip, of course, held a car coming the other way. The big Yamaha dived off the side of the road into the accommodating snowy ditch quite gracefully, I thought. Annie's

Camping at Senj restored our faith in the Yugoslav Mediterranean climate.

opinion was otherwise. The bloke in the car just shook his head.

We recovered with a terrific meal of roast pork and chips in a cafeteria above the bus station in Otocac and washed it down with a brandy (possibly sourced from the local hardware shop) before tackling the godforsaken plateau above Senj. It snowed again on the pass, but then we were through the weather and rolling down the twisting, lightly oiled and diesel soaked mountain road to the sea and sunshine.

We found a sweet little campsite on the water and it was actually warm enough to eat dinner outside the tent, although not quite warm enough for a dip. The rain came back the next day as we rolled into Dubrovnik and we couldn't resist the offer of a pension with a garage.

A German couple touring on an elderly BMW R60 joined us and we spent most of the evening telling stories over a few drinks. A lot of Germans seem to speak English, which is handy. A few days in Dubrovnik were a real pleasure. We did all the usual things - walks through the medieval city, around the walls and out to the fortress, as well as familiarising ourselves with Yugoslav cooking. There was a small bar tucked away in an alley down by the harbour that specialised in *burek*, the cheese or meat pastry. They also had *cevapcici* and *rasnici* (grilled meats) which I knew from Australia and we spent almost every evening there having a few beers with dinner.

An absolutely horrifying detour through the mountains claimed us as soon as we left Dubrovnik. The "road" was a more or less recently graded dirt track, and over the 40 or so kilometres it lasted we counted three trucks that had simply fallen off the roadway; two of them were lying on their sides, and one had rolled over onto its roof. The bike dealt with the surface quite well, due no doubt largely to the fat rear tyre, but there was chaos at the other end as cars and trucks squeezed past each other on the narrow cliff path. We were more than glad to be on the bike.

Just before Titograd we fell foul of a radar trap. For once, I actually had not been speeding, but you can't argue with Yugoslav traffic cops, even though their equipment was more than a little questionable.

"Our radar says you were speeding."

"That isn't a radar. It's a hairdryer." It was, too.

"It does not matter what it is," he snarled and wiggled his submachine gun suggestively. I paid the fine and rode on, seething. Still, if they caught me every time I do exceed the speed limit...

The Titograd campground had been vandalised badly since Charlie and I had stayed there 18 months before. The pretty lady wasn't in reception, either – in fact, there wasn't anybody in reception at all. I finally found someone at the hotel that adjoins the site and they told me to camp anywhere I liked, the site was open and free. Annie thought they just couldn't be bothered filling in all the forms. The watchman came past, cadged a couple of drinks, and promised to look after our tent extra carefully. I went to the bank to cash a travelers cheque and had to scribble my name on it four times before the teller was satisfied that my signature matched the sample.

Then on into darkest Yugoslavia, up hill and down dale on steadily worsening roads. We took the main road, not the track that Charlie and I had taken, but at times it wasn't much better. Winter had destroyed more than one bridge and undermined the road so often it was like a trials stage. In one tunnel there were great ice pillars, formed by water dripping from the ceiling, but we made it through to Skopje and then over quite passable back roads to Ohrid.

We heard a sad story that night in the cevapcici bar where we were having dinner. A young Yugoslav soldier came over to us and introduced himself in fluent Australian. He had been taken to Australia by his parents when he was two years old and had lived in Canberra for 16 years. Then he'd come back to see his relations and the army had grabbed him for two years" national service. They were pleased to get him since he had just passed his apprenticeship as a diesel mechanic, and they didn't have many of those. He had eight months to go, and was counting the days. "When I got here I didn't even speak the language", he told us sadly.

Our landlady gave us an heroic breakfast, including a gallon of coffee. Annie had washed a pair of her knickers and hung them on the back of the bike to dry, something we often did with wet clothes, and the landlady nearly cracked up. She thought it was the funniest thing she'd ever seen, and called out all the neighbours to share her glee.

The people at Bitola were helpful and pointed out the road to Greece, which was just as well as there wasn't a single road sign in the whole town.

CHAPTER 27

Greece Again

THERE WERE money-changing problems at the border (never change more money than you need) and the obstinate Greek Customs man wrote the bike into my passport, which was near to being full, instead of Annie's, which had more space. But you couldn't really stay annoyed long. Spring was with us at last – it had been following us all the way from Sicily, and now it was finally catching up.

After a run through fresh greenery we made camp at Meteora, below the famous rock cliffs like stone trolls with monasteries for hats and long trails of poo from the toilets overhanging the cliffs. We watched the tourist buses rolling up, and it struck me as odd that the monks should be able to reconcile the religious life with showing tourists around all day. Do they pray for a good tourist crop in between counting the admission money, I wonder?

> "Only we, contrary to the barbarians, never count the enemy in battle."
> AESCHYLUS

There was a large chrome and glass establishment in Kalabaka which advertised itself, in large day-glo letters and in English, as a "typical Greek taverna". What would Anthony Quinn have said?

Annie was befriended by a little black dog we nicknamed The Sheik for his habit of creeping into our tent when we were asleep. He followed her devotedly everywhere she went. The proprietor of the site didn't know who owned him. "He just likes tourists," he told us.

The Plain of Thessaly, although it sounds good, was dull. The excitement set in on the mountain road after Lamia, where a new road was being built and the old one had been sort of lost underneath, making it pretty rugged. At one point we stopped and were passed by a wartime German Zündapp outfit, pressed into service to

Sandwiches for lunch at Delphi put a smile on Annie's face.

deliver vegetables and elderly Greek ladies.

After passing the great olive grove of Itea, we climbed the cliff to Delphi and camped right on the edge of the drop. The scramble around the ruins was well worth it, but it's best timed for when the tourists are at lunch. Delphi is one of the prime sightseeing spots in the country and becomes badly crowded even in the off season.

We chatted to an elderly, tubby cop who was quite obviously in the grip of a lengthy love affair with his Harley-Davidson. He showed us where he'd painted this antediluvian monster himself, careful dabs of the brush over rust patches. A German arrived in the campsite one night on a shiny new BMW R45, still in shock from travelling on the Lamia road. We told him to try the Skopje-Titograd highway if he wanted a real experience. He was cheerfully horrified when he saw us loading the bike with all our worldly goods, and asked politely if he might take pictures. No doubt he's still scaring fellow motorcyclists with them, back in Germany.

The road to Thebes was fine, except that the surface deteriorated badly whenever we went through a town. Often town streets were dirt, not even gravel. Perhaps the powers that be feel that it's a waste of time tarring them – they'd only wear out again anyway...

On the motorway the radar caught us once more. This time I wasn't going to put up with any nonsense, and anyway I'm not scared of Greeks the way I am of Yugoslavs with submachine guns. I pointed out, at the top of my voice, that I had not been speeding as they appeared to claim, but only doing 100 on what was after all a freeway and didn't they have anything better to do? We were both still angry after the hairdryer episode and Annie joined in with my tirade. They eventually shooed us away, dazed by our combined assault. Around the next corner we found a sign indicating that the speed limit was 80...

Athens was, as always, dusty and noisy, with cancerous traffic. We picked up some mail, including a pair of visors kindly sent by Bob Heath and a note from the Mols saying that they'd be joining us a week later. That night, we were overcharged for our dinner of calamari down in Piraeus, and the waiter plied us with free retsina when we complained – we felt that we were getting this travelling business sorted out pretty damn well.

The week until Michel and Cathy arrived was spent exploring the Peloponnese. A couple of days lying in the sun at Epidaurus with an excursion to the well-preserved amphitheatre were followed by a visit to Sparta. Then we headed over the ranges to Kalamata and ran into more snow. It really is true; you become much more sensitive to nature's little quirks on a bike...

On Easter Sunday, the proprietor of the "Melbourne" cafe in Hora bought us some cakes and coffee. People kept giving us Easter presents all day – boiled eggs dyed red, biscuits and even a cucumber were thrust into our hands by people standing beside the road. Everyone was out in their front yards, roasting lambs on spits; the countryside smelt like a vast Greek restaurant. Olympia, which we'd intended to make the high spot of our day, had been closed by a strike. Back to reality!

On the tollway back to Athens, the toll collectors in their little hut waved us through for free, but it wasn't a good Easter for everyone. As we crested a hill, a puppy wandered out onto the roadway. I made a crash stop and Annie scooped it up, but its owners weren't to be seen. It had obviously been abandoned. We stood by the side of the road for a while holding it up as we'd seen people in Morocco do who wanted to sell pups, but nobody stopped. A puppy isn't a terribly sensible companion on a bike trip, especially when you have to cross borders. We really didn't know what to do. Finally, we took it along until we reached the outskirts of Athens, found a prosperous-looking suburb and dumped it on someone's front lawn. We assumed that its chances would be better there than on the motorway. But as we drew away, it was already tottering back out onto the road. A sad end to Easter, both for the pup (I presume) and us.

We set up camp, bought some wine and sat around feeling miserable. The next day we had trouble at the bank and begrudged the Bulgarians their extortionate fee for a 30-hour visa. A pall descended that wasn't broken until the Mols arrived, grinning from ear to ear.

Michel and Cathy had left London in the cold and drizzling rain, and had had much the same weather until southern Germany, when the snow had started. On the autobahn to Austria, they had been riding through snowdrifts and had camped in them in Salzburg. Finally out of the heavy weather on the Yugoslav coast, they had had a slight argument with a large pointed rock which had bent their front rim and flattened the tyre. Michel had bashed the wheel back into shape with his axe, replaced the tube and they'd ridden on. And they were cheerful when they arrived in Athens!

We rolled out the plastic jug of retsina and sat down for a little party. It was good to see them again. The hangovers in the morning were something to behold, except for Annie. She's the only person I know who knows her limit – most of the time anyway. We packed up rather gingerly and then flew up the motorway. None of the speed traps were interested in us. The strain of keeping up with the R100S showed on the Yamaha's worn-out shock absorbers, and I wallowed around the corners the BMW was taking in style.

The weather was deteriorating again, but we got away from it by spending a couple of days on Thasos. This island is less than an hour from the mainland by ferry and specialises in honey and having its roads sink into the sea. It's a pretty, pine-covered place and has a good campsite as well as miles of coastline suitable for free camping. We had a barbecue on the beach, using a suntan lotion shop display rack as a griddle, and sank a few beers. Then it was time for a run around the island, checking out the sunken roads – there were several places where you could have gone skindiving without leaving the saddle – and back to the mainland.

On the way up to Alexandropoulis, over those pretty mountain roads, a police car came the other way around a corner while I was way over the centre line – they didn't bat an eye as I corrected and drew sparks from my centre stand. The rack on the XS had developed a couple of cracks in North Africa when we had overloaded it so badly, and these were getting worse. Reluctantly, I decided we wouldn't be able to carry spare petrol in Turkey.

We had another game of hunt-the-gas bottle for our little cooker. You can buy the cartridges everywhere, and you can generally buy large caravan-size bottles, but the little ones are hard to find. A kindly German-speaking cab driver finally took us around the town looking for one, for free, and found it. A knowledge of German is invaluable in Greece and Turkey, as so many people have worked in Germany. Our cab driver, for instance, had saved enough money while working there to buy his cab, which he had then driven home to Greece.

CHAPTER 28

Turkey Again

THE ROAD TO the border was indifferent and the service on the Greek side quick if not exactly courteous. The Turks were working at their usual pace – dead slow – and held us up for a while, but at least there weren't any Customs searches. The road down towards Gallipoli was initially quite good and for a while I thought we were in the wrong country, but it soon deteriorated, and the Mols took flying lessons on a tricky humpbacked bridge. We had lunch there and a German couple, he on an XS1100, she on a CX500, stopped and told us that a few years earlier they had managed to get a 2CV Renault airborne on that bridge.

"And you. When will you begin that long journey into yourself? When?"

JALALUDDIN RUMI

We had intended to have a look at the site of the infamous Gallipoli landings of the First Great Unpleasantness, but couldn't find any cliffs that looked likely. Later

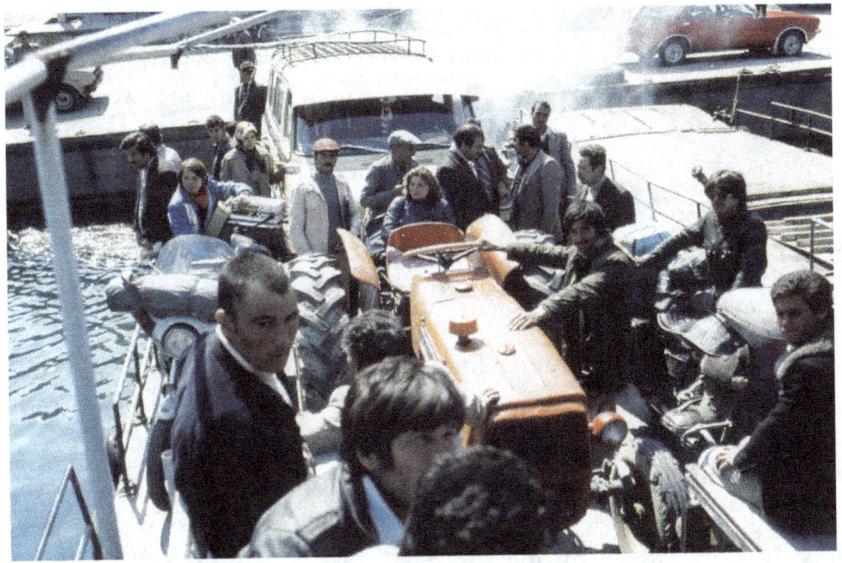

This is the ferry that took us across from Europe to Asia in Turkey. Interesting.

we found out that the landings hadn't been at Gallipoli at all, but on the other side of the peninsula. No wonder it was a disaster.

The ferry to Canakkale in Asia Minor had just left when we arrived at the wharf – it was only running intermittently due to a diesel shortage – so we were facing a three-and-a-half hour wait. A man at the wharf told us about a local ferry that ran from a place a little farther down the coast; I wish he hadn't tried to help. This local ferry was a mildly converted fishing boat, with extremely flimsy water pipe rails and nothing to tie the bikes to. We shared it with a defunct tractor and a van, and it was so crowded that the bikes were right on the edge. We hung onto them for grim death all the way across the Dardanelles. It would have taken only one largish wave...

Past rows of closed campsites – the season hadn't started in Turkey – we rode to Troy for a look at the ruins. The place is quite a mess. Apparently there are numerous Troys, one above the other, and it's all a bit of a chore sorting it out. It is very impressive, though, to see several thousand years of civilisation in a few yards of hillside. You'll be glad to know that the wooden horse is still there. You can even climb up inside and play Greeks and Trojans.

On the way back to the main road, a kid lobbed a rock at us. My feelings about this kind of thing hadn't changed since the last time it had happened, in Afghanistan. I turned around and went back with the motor on the red line in first. The kid ran as though all the demons in hell were after him, and I guess the big Yamaha sounded a bit like that. I caught him and gave him a dressing down in front of his mates. A bit self-righteous, maybe, but if it stops him and his friends from throwing stones at other bikes it will have been worth it. So there.

Lots of pretty hill country then, and for the night a tiny campsite marked "Kampink-Piknik". It was quite idyllic, but they'd run out of beer. I guess no place is ever perfect.

The BBC World Service news on my little short-wave radio was cheerful and informed us that three people had died in political shootings in Turkey during the day and that a military coup was

The Trojan Horse has withstood the ravages of time rather well, I thought.

starting. I'm glad to say that nobody has ever shot at me – well, not for a good long time, anyway – and nobody shot at any of us in Turkey. I told the manager of the campsite about the military coup, and he said he hadn't heard about it and anyway who cared. Next morning we had to search for a while before finding a petrol station that would sell us juice, not because there was a shortage of petrol but because the electricity was off. Not all stations have hand pumps.

At one place we looked like being out of luck when three Italian campervans pulled in behind us. A bevy of bikini-clad young women exploded from the vans, and all of a sudden petrol was available after all, even if it had to be pumped by hand.

The road to Izmir reminded me of Greece. As soon as you got into the town limits, the tar stopped and the gravel started. After Izmir we were on the main road again and diced with the buses and trucks down past Ephesus to the coast at Kusadasi. The town is a port of call for many of the cruise liners that ply the Mediterranean and prices in town go up between 100 and 2000 per cent whenever ships are in port. We learnt to do our shopping after they had left.

There were some attractive bike leathers for sale here and I was tempted, but they weren't all that much cheaper than in Britain, and you get after-sales service in Britain. We lay in the sun for a bit, and I bolted the stays from the top box onto the bike frame instead of the rack. Not quite so elegant, but it put less strain on the cracks.

Going inland, we followed the country lanes for a while, riding through the little villages dozing in the sun, before we returned to the main road and the traffic. At Pamukkale, an area of hot springs and calcium deposits that turn whole hillsides white with dozens of stepped warm pools, we camped in a tiny site with a large pool. The pool was bigger than the camping area.

Our host was a keen man after a buck, as a lot of Turks are (and you can't blame them), and we had a classic run-in with him. Michel priced the beer, an essential step if you don't want to find yourself with an enormous bill. He was quoted 40 lire for a bottle. We both hit the roof, as 30 is considered expensive, and our genial host backpedaled rapidly. "Oh, you want the beer for *drinking!* That's only 30."

The frogs in the pool did their best to keep us awake and there was an attempt to short-change us in the morning, but other than that, Pamukkale was a pleasant place. On the way out of town the clutch on the BMW started slipping quite badly, but Michel adjusted it up as far as possible and managed to make the bike rideable.

The road we had selected to take us back to the coast was marked as "stabilised" beyond the little town of Kale on our map. In Kale, we stopped for a glass of tea and Annie and Cathy were the only women in the tea house. No-one appeared to be concerned. We donned rain gear, and the locals tried to dissuade us from going on. "Rocks this big and mud that deep!" they said. They were right, too; "stabilised" turned out to mean deep, gluey mud and we lasted a little more than a mile before deciding it wasn't for us. That road was 56 miles long!

Our alternative was better, and a filling lunch of *kofte* (meatballs) and beans was enlivened by a conversation with a couple of bank tellers, who were delighted to exercise their English. They told us that petrol prices had doubled in the previous month. We still thought it cheap.

On the road down through the ranges, Michel suddenly pulled over to the left and stopped. I followed, put the side stand down – and the bike fell over on the slope. The stand had broken through the tar, and the bike tipped, spilling Annie and me off – right under the back wheel of the BMW. Now Michel had pulled over because he thought he smelled something burning. His first thought, therefore, when I dived under the back of his bike, was that I was putting out a fire. So he dived off as well, also ready to extinguish the blaze. Confusion reigned for a minute until we had it all sorted out, the XS back on its wheels and Michel reassured that the R100 wasn't about to go up in smoke. Annie then saved the day by producing the brandy flask. Those Vetter fairings really are good – better than any crashbar – and there's room for a brandy flask in the pocket. There wasn't a scratch on the XS.

We found a campsite out at Kemer, past Antalya – it was free because the season hadn't started ("No, no", said the site manager, that meant only that he couldn't charge us, not that we couldn't stay; in fact he turned on the hot water for the showers) – and we did a bit more lying around in the sun, as well as going for a run down the coast to Kas. This stretch was as pretty as ever with its steep, pine-covered hills and empty beaches. The road that was being built when Charlie and I had come through here a year and a half before was already disintegrating.

The Yamaha handled the potholes and gravel noticeably better than the BMW, despite the stuffed shocks. The BMW also had a flat tyre on the morning of our departure. Nothing to do with Turkey, this was an after-effect of the encounter with the rock in Yugoslavia. The tyre had sustained a slight split on the inside, and this had been plucking away at the tube, finally tearing it. I'll say this for BMW, they supply an excellent pump.

After another ethnic lunch at Antalya, we rolled east along the rather featureless coast. In Anamur, the bikes were parked on an embankment above the market square while we did some shopping,

Camping at Pamukkale, and buying beer "for drinking".

There are remnants of Crusader castles all along the Mediterranean coast of Turkey.

but suddenly a gust of wind caught the BMW and flipped it onto its side. The bike landed right on the edge of the embankment, slipped over and crashed down a foot and a half onto its back on concrete. Then it tipped onto its side. Almost a complete somersault. At first it looked as though the only damage was a broken mirror and a cracked fairing, but when we tried to ride away the back tyre was rubbing against the guard. The fall had bent the rear frame loop.

Fortunately, another campsite presented itself just down on the beach. When the owner realised that we were having problems with the bike, he told us his friend had the tools to fix that, ands would be around in the morning. He then invited us to dinner and drinks. A thoroughly drunken night followed: we tried to teach our host some Australian songs (no, no, once a jolly swagman…); he recited a great deal of poetry, we did some dancing; there were drunken protestations of eternal friendship; and in an incredibly badly judged display of helpfulness I gave two guys a lift home high into the hills on the big Yammie – both of them on the back at the same time on single track paths alongside irrigation canals. After I delivered them I had no idea where I was. Well, actually I knew where I was. I just didn't know where anywhere else was. I navigated by the lights of the town down by the water.

Annie misjudged the strength of the spirits and went to sleep in my lap when I finally got back, and what eventually saved us was the nearby shop running out of raki. We had to switch to the considerably less alcoholic beer. I've seldom had such a good time.

We "repaired" the R100S in the morning with the special tools our drinking buddy's friend had – a couple of enormous crowbars – took a look at the marvelous Crusader castle while our hangovers abated and then tackled the cliff road east. This is a great run through stunning country, made less pleasant only by the lumbering timber trucks. We had trouble keeping up with the flying Mols as the BMW's handling came into its own on the tar. Camp was at the BP Mocamp that Charlie and I had disliked so heartily on the previous occasion. Everyone wanted a shower. The place was still as expensive and the

Some Turkish roads are a little on the muddy side.

staff as rude as before, but at least the water was hot.

Then on to Mersin, where a tractor tried to run Michel off the road, and up through the Cilician Gates to the Anatolian Plateau. The dual carriageway claimed by our map turned out to be sheer optimism – all they'd done was make the old road less passable with their road works.

The Rock House Hotel at Goreme was closed, perhaps because it was still early in the season, so we went to "Paris" Camping instead, which not only had hot showers but free gas cookers and tables and chairs. A few days passed pleasantly enough with sightseeing and clambering in and out of stone houses, and we changed the rear tyre on the XS without any of the problems experienced by the bike shop in France. Well, getting the bead on the tyre to pop properly wasn't easy with only a hand pump, but the security bolts gave no trouble at all.

We climbed to the top of the stone fortress at Uchisar, and one of the town urchins chased us all the way up to sell us a guide book.

Unfortunately, he'd gone by the bikes – full German registration on the Yamaha and German tax-free registration on the BMW – and had brought the German guidebook instead of the English one; a wasted climb.

On the way to Ankara via Kirsehir everything was green again. The fields and meadows were feeling the spring even here on the high plateau. Crossing an embankment, the Mols hit a pothole and bombed the unsuspecting peasants below with one of their panniers – the Krauser came off the bike, bounced along the road and then dived down into the fields, but there was no damage beyond a few scratches. Now you know why BMW riders with old Krauser panniers always have straps around them. The main road to Ankara hadn't improved since I'd last travelled it and we had to contend with long stretches of gravel and dirt. The Ankara campground had taken down its sign, but I remembered where it was and we managed to wake the guard. Although my old friend Rochester had gone, we were still not allowed to camp on the grass, just like old times. When we went off to do a little shopping, we discovered that a kilo of onions cost the same as six bottles of beer. There's a moral there somewhere.

It was back out into the gray air and heavy traffic of Ankara in the morning. Martial law was in operation, every corner had its soldiers, and at strategic intersections there were rows of tanks. The tank crews were really taken with the bikes and waved enthusiastically as we passed. We waved back, of course. Of course!

Suddenly the BMW started to lose oil rapidly, and it didn't take long to find out why. The sump was gradually lowering itself on its bolts and spitting out oil. Michel tightened it, making ominous comments about Turkey and BMWs. Then we were off to do battle with the traffic on the Istanbul road. The less said about this run the better – we were forced off the road once each and didn't really enjoy it. The first tanks at the outskirts of Istanbul were actually a welcome sight, and when we stopped the crew of one of them insisted on giving us cigarettes. Soon afterwards, we rolled over the toll bridge back into Europe.

We located the most convenient camping ground, set up the tents and ducked off to town for dinner; I took the others to the little kebab bar Charlie and I had found, where the food was as good as ever.

We resealed the sump on the R100S with liquid gasket and I put the stays from the top box back into their proper place on the rack. I thought we were through the worst of the roads; little did I know.

After the obligatory rounds of sightseeing, which are more worthwhile in Istanbul than in most places, we raided the Grand Bazaar. It sells everything from everywhere – all at negotiable prices. Never believe what the merchants tell you, just dig in and enjoy it. They have some beautiful things – I bought Annie a miniature painting on ivory (yes, I know, ivory – but it was clearly quite old and the elephant would have died a long time ago) and myself a pipe, an eagle's claw carved out of meerschaum. The radio featured marvelous selections from sixties and seventies rock as well as classical music, and we played a chess championship. I won! But only because all the others were even more beginners than I. An idyllic existence, despite martial law and shootings.

Then the Mols were off again to southern Greece and the sun, carrying with them our Scrabble set as a farewell gift. We turned our wheels towards Bulgaria and then home. The trip had lasted over six months by this stage and we were quite happy to have it end. A tour has a sort of natural lifespan, although most people have to get back to work before it runs for that long. The lifespan of our tour was coming to an end, and it was time to let it die gracefully.

CHAPTER 29

The Eastern Bloc and back to England

> *"It would not frighten me if I were to lose my throne. If that were to happen, I would go right to America and get a job as a mechanic."*
>
> **BORIS III OF BULGARIA**

THE CUSTOMS man at the Bulgarian border asked us for third-party insurance, which we no longer had. When I told him this, he rolled his eyes heavenwards and waved us through – he couldn't be bothered getting the forms out. Bulgarian roads were pretty nasty, mostly cobblestoned and wavier than the Bay of Biscay in a gale. Someone once said that the potholes were the size of small planets. Big moons, maybe. Fields were being ploughed by small tractors with treads instead of wheels, possibly lightly converted tanks. We felt our way gingerly through the forested hills to Veliko Tarnovo. The campsite there turned out to be the most expensive of the trip, but at least it had plenty of hot water for the showers, although I cannot for the life of me imagine why the taps were electrified...

Perhaps some of the cost of the site was an entertainment charge. We were certainly entertained, by singing and revelry, until about 2.30am. It was a party of East Germans who were no doubt glad to be away from the Stasi. We in our turn were glad to get out of Bulgaria after our extensive stay of 30 hours – that was all the time our visa gave us. Good thing, too. Among other things, the roads had finally done what even the Yugoslav ones had not managed – they had broken the bike's luggage rack.

Romanian Customs must have had us pegged as International Drug Runners. They searched everything on and off the bike, even

Bulgaria was not the most charming of places, but we found some nice little chalets.

though their drug-sniffing dog didn't show the slightest interest in us. The highlight of the ceremony came when one of the male customs officers found a suspicious small cardboard box filled with what looked like miniature white sticks of explosive, with fuse attached. Neither of us spoke Romanian, and Annie finally got through with a bit of French.

"*Pour Madame,*" she said. The customs officer looked at the box of tampons, went bright red and couldn't give them back quickly enough.

We then had to change $10 per day of our visit into the local currency and should also, apparently, have bought petrol coupons. Nobody told us anything about them, so we rode blithely off. As it turned out, only one petrol station asked for them, and they filled our tank anyway when we shrugged our shoulders. The roads were noticeably better than the ones in Bulgaria, and we made it to Bucharest for lunch. We ate at the Carul cu Bere, a restaurant in an 18th-century inn. The food here was superb, beer came in great stoneware steins and was delicious, and it was all quite cheap. I know the people were being oppressed by the government, but everyone we saw seemed cheerful enough – even the ones eating the awful greasy ice cream. Ben and Jerry's, Romania is yours for the taking.

It was frustrating trying to find somewhere to camp. Most of the sites listed in the official booklet (another damned official booklet) were either closed or had disappeared. One was even closed for stocktaking!

"One tree, check. Grass, sort of, 80 square metres, check. Pile of gravel, one of. Where's the pile of gravel, Karoly?"

When we finally found a site the bike immediately attracted a crowd of truck drivers. While they were admiring the twin disc brakes up front, one drew me aside. He told me that he was Hungarian, and to be sure to lock everything up. The Romanians, it seemed, were all thieves. Marvelous, I thought. Later a Romanian told me that Hungarians would sell their grandmothers for a packet of cigarettes. Why do neighbours always delight in blackening each other's names?

This slanderous tendency isn't restricted to morals. When I made a disparaging remark about the Bulgarian roads, all the Romanians were tickled. One of them pointed to the dirt track we were on and suggested that that was what the Bulgarian roads were like. I said no, worse, and he pointed to the ploughed field next to the campsite. When I nodded, they roared with laughter and then bought us beer.

We had a race with a diesel locomotive up into the Transylvanian Alps and lost when we came to a red light. It was unfair – there was no red light for the train. These mountains are beautiful and full of old chateaux and grand hotels from the days before Communism. Most of them had been turned into workers' holiday hostels – one improvement, anyway. We saw no signs of direct bloodsucking.

Somewhere in the north of Romania we lost the rubber plug out of the cam chain tensioner. I manufactured a new one from rolled-up adhesive tape and wired it into place – it seemed to do the job very nicely. We were once again trying to find a replacement gas bottle, and in Oradea near the Hungarian border finally found a gas depot. It was closed, but there were some people outside and one of them took

More chalets in Romania, but we chose to stick with our tent.

our empty bottle, passed it through the fence to somebody inside and got a new one back for us, free of charge. Nice people everywhere, or maybe they just enjoy sticking a thumb into Authority's eye.

The border with Hungary was easy, except that once again we had trouble changing unwanted money back. It's against the law to take Romanian money out of the country but they wouldn't give us anything else, so we had to spend our remaining cash on the el cheapo souvenir wooden plates with pokerwork decorations which were the only things for sale. Could this have been deliberate?

The roads to Budapest were smooth and straight and almost unbelievably flat. With conservative and polite drivers as well, Hungary is one of the most pleasant countries in Europe to ride in, although things weren't quite so easy in Budapest. Annie checked with the Tourist Bureau and they told her that the campsite was closed, which seemed a bit unlikely to us. We rode out there just to make sure and lo! not only was it open, but it was open the whole year round, and it was a pleasant enough site despite the loud disco music from the restaurant at night. Isn't it great to see Western culture spread behind the Iron Curtain?

Budapest has excellent public transport and is an altogether prosperous city. The people still didn't look happy though, and the truckloads of Russian soldiers we saw were pointedly ignored. We took the road along the Danube on our way to the Austrian border and were rewarded by quiet country lanes and lush greenery. The border was quick as they were only searching cars, not bikes. There's a tip there, unless they change over on even days... As we rode into Vienna that afternoon, the back wheel of the Yamaha started making the most peculiar scraping noise. I tracked it down to a shoelace caught in the rear brake caliper.

An overnight stay in Vienna, in a clean and well-equipped campsite, and we were on our way again – no more time for sightseeing. The border with Germany is a one-stop affair – the guards showed our passports to a computer, which raised no objections, and we were simultaneously out and in. Coming into Passau, we started chatting to a bloke on an ancient BMW outfit, and he showed us a good pub for lunch.

We camped in Nuremberg that night, near the stadium made famous by the big Nazi rallies. It's a parking lot now, which seems appropriate. The campsite was excellent, as all German campsites seem to be. Then it was up the Autobahn, on to Brunswick and a few days with relatives. Then a long day across to Ostend and the late ferry to Dover. Due to delays on the ferry - it kept yo-yoing around in Dover harbour - and problems with the ramp, we didn't get ashore until well after midnight. The Customs man asked us where we'd been and wasn't at all impressed by the 18 countries I rattled off. He just asked whether we'd picked up any "noxious substances" and when we said no, we didn't think so, let us go.

Miracles do still happen. There was a bed-and-breakfast place still open on the Folkestone road, and the first thing our landlady did was offer us a cup of tea. We were back in England, all right.

The run to London was just a formality. We were back, 194 days, 20,000 miles and £2000 after we'd set out. A great trip, albeit with its ups and downs. And then there was the next one…

PART 3

Home Through America

CHAPTER 30

The North

*"America will never be destroyed from the outside.
If we falter and lose our freedoms,
it will be because we destroyed ourselves."*

ABRAHAM LINCOLN

WE WERE IN brilliant sunlight at 30,000 feet as the Laker DC10 started its descent into John F. Kennedy Airport. Fifteen minutes later, on the ground, it was night – darkness broken only by the beacon of the dozens of aircraft milling around waiting to park or take off. I found myself hoping fervently that this was not going to be an omen for my long-awaited tour of the US. Half an hour later my fears were firming up.

The immigration lines in the arrivals lounge were long, slow and staffed by people obviously bored with their job of keeping America safe for democracy. I got short shrift – two months to be precise – when I tried to get an entry permit to take me up to the date on my onward ticket – all of three weeks later than the two months.

But – America, land of contrasts! – things were quite different at Customs. Not only did the officer disdain to search my luggage, but as soon as he noticed that I was a motorcyclist – easily deduced from the crash helmet under my arm – he engaged me in a lengthy and interesting discussion of bike usage in the US. He then closed his station and went off to find out the easiest and cheapest way in which I might recover my bike, which had come by airfreight, out of bond.

There are two types of Americans, I have come to realise. Those who can't do too much for you, and those who can't do anything for you.

Ten minutes later, equipped with detailed – though unfortunately wrong – information, as well as the address and phone number of my first American friend, I boarded the bus into Gotham City. For $5 the airport bus was good value. You get to goggle out at the fascinating and scary concrete ribbons of the freeways, contemplate the towering housing projects and quickly summarise all the warnings about New York - while you're still safe. As soon as you step out of the bus at the Lower East Side Bus Terminal you're on your own. At 1.00am, for me, this seemed about on a par with crossing Parramatta Road (Sydney's main traffic artery) at 5.00pm on a Friday afternoon. Death lurked everywhere.

I didn't have any American change, so one of the taxi drivers - a sizeable black person - lent me a dime to ring the Youth Hostel. They didn't answer, so I decided to go round and wake them up. The loan of ten cents had put me so much in the moral debt of my driver that I didn't feel able to protest his charge of $8.50 for ten city blocks... He did me a favour by pointing out that I was in one of the toughest neighbourhoods in Manhattan, and to watch out. If anyone tried to "put trouble on me", he suggested I keep walking. I amended that to "running" and thanked him.

The hostel was closed for the night, of course, but I got a room in the hotel next door, as well as a much appreciated snack in the hotel's all night coffee shop. The bellboy pointed out that the TV would operate only if the bathroom light was switched on; I gave him a dollar and fell into bed.

I am a creature of sunshine. The next morning, with temperatures climbing towards the century mark they reached every day while I was in New York, I felt immeasurably better and more in control. I checked in at the hostel, stowed my baggage and went out for a walk. As I left the hostel, my eye was caught by the unmistakable shape of the Empire State Building, visible through a gap between some other buildings across the road. I stopped and admired it for a moment, then turned and began to walk on.

"Hey, buddy." A well-dressed black bloke standing in a doorway marked "NY Community College" called me over. "Buddy, I been workin' here for 20 years. Ever' now and then, folk stop where you did an' look up in the air. What you lookin' at?" I motioned for him to come back a few steps with me, to where he could see the Empire State, and pointed.

"The Empire State?" he said. "Oh, yeah, sure. The Empire State. Yeah. Never thought o' that..." I'm still not sure if he was taking the piss. Well, actually I am.

It was beginning to get muggy, even early in the morning, and I turned up towards Central Park. It's a blast walking through New York. I doubt that there's a more interesting place on Earth. And it's all the people; the diversity, the style, the craziness. In Central Park, this being summer, it was all hanging out. I have never seen so many scantily covered ample breasts and buttocks in my life – and most of them on wheels, too. Roller skates everywhere, people with radios clamped to their heads bopping, rolling, even dancing ... and rippling – the males with muscles, the females mainly with, er ... other tissue.

The remainder of those couple of days is a bit of a blur. There was Greenwich Village, with the frisbee experts working out in Washington Square; the great food in the delis; the spectacular comics pages the Sunday papers serve up; the sight of miles and miles of smog from the top of the Empire State; Waylon Jennings at the Lone Star for $1 cover charge; and the terrible beer.

I approached the beer scientifically. One evening, I bought one can each of six different beers and retreated to the room I shared with a swarthy Frenchman and two melancholy Danes. As I listened to tales of touring the US and Canada by BMW – this from the Frenchman, who'd shipped his bike over and spent eight weeks buzzing around – I sampled the brews. They were all awful, without exception. Pale, flavourless and nearly non-alcoholic, they all tasted the same. Bad sign.

One of the Danes explained his melancholia, too. He had, it seemed, been mugged. His papers, money and travellers cheques had been taken – in Miami, of all places. I'd always thought of Miami as a sort of geriatric anteroom to a morgue, but it seemed street crime

Ready to reassemble the XL at the warehouse; this time the airline did supply the pallet.

was a problem. For the Dane, anyway. His consulate, fortunately, had come to the rescue. They had replaced his passport on the spot and had lent him some money.

With the mugging story still fresh in my mind, I descended into the subways to make my way out to suburban Jamaica to pick up the freight papers for the bike. Graffiti on the NY trains is of a very high standard, and the trains themselves are occasionally even air-conditioned. Papers in hand, I presented myself at the freight depot. It seemed that some mud had been noticed under the guards on the bike, so the Department of Agriculture man had to be called. Foreign mud is a no-no. I sat around, gasping in the heat, for an hour or so until he came. After one look, he decided that he wasn't worried. Ah, mud shmud. I was then free to deal with the lady from Customs, who suspected everyone and everything – she gave me a hard time because my bike registration papers had expired, but finally relented. She did not mention insurance, fortunately.

So I had the bike back – rather bent, since someone had dropped a crate on it, but still my bike. I had to straighten the shock absorbers with a crowbar, but the rest of it wasn't too bad and went back together quite well. It wouldn't start, though; throwing away the contents of the float bowl and pushing finally did the trick. My grateful thanks to the guys at Seaboard World, who donated a gallon of petrol and then pushed. I couldn't have done it without ya.

My first encounter with the freeway system, on the way back into Manhattan, wasn't reassuring. The signs were so cryptic. What do I know from 72nd Street? Signposting is all very local, unless you've memorised the route numbers. No denying that the freeways get you around at a great rate of knots, though. I was back at the hostel before I knew it. I fitted my lovely new Oxford Fairings windscreen out in the street, and attracted all sorts of loonies. One of them insisted on telling me the long, dreary and predictable story of the disintegration of his Gold Star BSA.

There are British bikes slowly corroding and dying all over the world. I know this because I have been told many times.

With the bike locked to a light pole, I went out for another night on the town. Once again, there were no dire consequences in the morning because the American beer is simply too mild to cause hangovers and I only had a few bourbons. That morning saw me stuck on the freeway within minutes of leaving the hostel. There had been a downpour, and half the road was under water – the half going my way, of course. Finally, on the way out to upper New York State, the buildings gave way to greenery. All of New England turned out to be surprisingly lush, which was still new to me at this stage. New York State looked rather as I'd imagined Louisiana.

I made my way north to Old Forge in the next few days. In Kingston, in the obligatory aluminium diner (run here by a Vietnamese family), I encountered "Doc", the head of the town emergency services. This includes ambulance, fire brigade and rescue. He was an ex-Marine Colonel, and insisted on giving me an enormous Marines badge sticker, a small American flag and a free breakfast. The hostel in Old Forge was equipped with a large group of bicycling Canadian nymphets, who entertained me splendidly during my stay. They even fed me.

My petrol tank, once broken in Malaysia and often repaired, had been cracked again during the flight. I had to glue it up once again after I had noticed petrol running down over the hot engine. I turned east then, to head for Vermont and later the coast. By now I was learning to navigate by route numbers and had no trouble finding my way about. I picked up a bit of sunburn buzzing around the little lakes and extensive forests of New England, and didn't mind one bit. It was beautiful and serene country, bathed in sunlight – with just the occasional thunderstorm and downpour to keep it interesting.

Concord didn't impress me so much. The home of one of my very few heroes (actually, even then I was beginning to have second thoughts about him), Henry David Thoreau, it was far from the small town surrounded by forest that he described last century. Now, it was a particularly nasty urban sprawl, reminding me of nothing quite so much as the Latrobe Valley in southern Victoria, one of my least favourite places. But then Concord hadn't been Concord even in

It seems they've heard of me in New England, but I'm not sure about the politics.

Thoreau's day, and he had cheated on that stay in the woods anyway...

That night, after tightening the chain on the bike for the third time, I finally discovered a reasonably drinkable beer. It was called Molson's, came from Canada and at least had some flavour. Still no strength, though. This was turning out to be a relaxed, lazy sort of swing through pretty countryside, rather different from the America I'd been led to expect. Even Boston, my first big city outside New York, seemed a laid-back place to me. I drifted through on the main roads, stopped for a cup of coffee at the Transportation Museum, and then carried on towards Cape Cod.

A group of three Canadian bikers passed me and then stopped to have a look at the XL. In honour of America, I had dubbed it "Hardly Davidson", and these blokes thought that was very funny. Mind you, they were on a Z750, a GS850 and a Z1000. They could afford to laugh.

It was misty all the way out to Cape Cod, so I couldn't admire much scenery, but there was enough to admire by the side of the road, anyway. Everybody was having a garage sale – some of the stuff people were unloading really tempted me. There were a couple of Buddy Holly albums, for example, in near-perfect condition, for only $2 each. Two bucks!

Once at the Orleans, Massachusetts, hostel, I took the tank off the bike, scraped off the liquid gasket with which I'd tried to stop the leak, and re-glued it with acrylic glue, which seemed to do the trick.

Crossing the high bridge at Newport, Rhode Island, brought to mind the grace of the yachts during the Americas Cup, and the film "Jazz on a Summer's Day", made here during one of the real Newport Jazz Festivals. It's weird; we see so much of America on TV and in the movies that it's quite possible to feel nostalgic entering a town you've never been to.

On my way up to the hills of Connecticut I stopped off for some of the dreadful, gummy American bread. When I came out of the supermarket, the bike was leaking petrol once again. This time it came from the carburettor breather pipe. I whipped the float bowl off, bent the float down and reassembled the carburettor. No more leak. Some time later, I looked down to find that the tank had split again, and petrol was dribbling onto the engine once more. I stopped at a hardware store and bought a two-phase adhesive called Liquid Steel that contained, according to the box, "real steel". I wasn't going to have any more backchat from this bike! I glued up the tank and the tap, which was weeping very slightly, and gave the bike as complete an overhaul as I, with my severely limited mechanical ability, could; I didn't discover any further problems.

It was back to NY then to check for mail and amble around a little more. In the footsteps of Walt Whitman, I took the Staten Island ferry and was impressed by the Manhattan skyline from the water. Then I rang Road Rider magazine in California for the dates of the Aspencade Motorcycle Convention, a "do" I had hoped to get to for years, and planned my trip across the USA. Very vaguely, I might add. I just knew I wanted to be in Ruidoso, New Mexico, on 1 October. That gave me some eight weeks.

Up and away then. Out through the Holland Tunnel the next morning, the bike was running rather rough. I had visions of breaking down in the tunnel – there's nowhere to park – and being fined vast sums of money. But the bike kept running, and as soon as I was out of the tunnel and switched off the headlight, the engine smoothed out. *Aha! Middle-aged XL Disease*, I thought. One of the symptoms is lack of electricity being generated, and the bike can't even run its pitiful headlight. Mechanical menopause approaching here. Then on down the ribbon of car yards, cheap motels and gas stations that is Highway One until I got hopelessly lost in roadworks in Baltimore looking for fuel. A thoroughly depressing city, it sticks out in my mind for the obvious poverty and overwhelming friendliness of its mostly black population. I mean, think about it – here's a white boy on a motorsickle, stopping to ask directions from the bros deep in the 'hood, and they say "What you doin' here? You best git your gas and you git gone, my man!"

Washington provided the Smithsonian Institution, where I

Repairing the tank once again. I finally got it to hold fuel with Liquid Steel.

I didn't realise you could get this close to the White House with your motorcycle!

admired Buzz Aldrin's toothbrush and touched a piece of the moon; the Star Wars subway, very efficient and pretty; and drinks at Matt Kane's bar. This last proved to be the most interesting, as I had a few drinks with the pilot of Air Force One, the presidential jet, and listened to his Washington gossip. It's true, he gave me a book of Air Force One matches! I've still got them here somewhere. Other than that Washington was not pleasant. For a national capital it's remarkably run down. Brothels and sex shops flourish within a couple of blocks of the White House, and there's an atmosphere of menace.

CHAPTER 31

The South

It was much better when I got out of town. I rode up the Potomac, and then followed the line of the Chesapeake and Ohio Canal. This is now a national park and is maintained for walkers, canoeists and bicyclists. It seemed as though there were thousands of butterflies, all keen to commit suicide on my windscreen or legs. That night was my first camp. I'd finally run out of Youth Hostels. So of course I had a thunderstorm and nearly an inch of rain in three hours. Huddled in my little tent (I'd bought it for $10 from some Swiss blokes in the Gol-e-Sahra campsite in Tehran), I consoled myself with the thought that the enormous caravans and mobile homes parked all around would be far more likely to draw the lightning than my little XL. I finally fell asleep while the thunder was still muttering to itself over the Shenandoah Hills.

> *"Save your Confederate money, boys. The South will rise again!"*
> **POPULAR SONG (IN THE SOUTH)**

Over breakfast, I got an explanation of the mysterious term "scrapple" that had started to appear on menus. "Wal," said the chef, "yo biles up various parts of th' insahde o' th' hawg, let it cool and then slahce an' frah it..." Um. I stuck to bacon and eggs, over easy.

The Blue Ridge Parkway was next, a bit of road every bit as pretty as its name. Parkways have no advertising on them, don't allow trucks, follow the contours of the land and are administered by the National Parks Service. This one follows the Blue Ridge Mountains for some 500 miles, all of it lovely, with the Appalachians rolling off to both sides like waves in an enormous, ancient slow ocean.

The Morgans, from Danby, Pennsylvania, pulled up while I was trying to take a photo of the forests, and asked about my Australian number plate. They also volunteered a beer and insisted that I take down their address and come and stay next time I was around Danby.

I accepted gladly. Americans are certainly a friendly lot, rather like the Irish, and much more friendly than the British or Australians.

Although I didn't manage to see any of the bears that supposedly inhabit the park, I felt quite ridiculously happy all day, sang little songs and waved at all the Honda Gold Wings, Harleys and Kawasaki Z1300s that went past. They all waved back, although some of them were clearly puzzled by my bike. I stayed with friends of friends in Boone that night, which had the distinction of being my first dry town in the USA. We had to drive eight miles to get across the county line and find a bar where we could spend the rest of the evening drinking jugs of Black & Tan.

The countryside in Georgia was dull and mostly flat. So much for the moonlight through the pines.

Atlanta promised to be a bit more interesting when I discovered that the Youth Hostel had been demolished – and there certainly weren't any campsites around. I stayed in the YMCA downtown. When I went for an after dinner walk, I was the only white person on the street although I was so naïve that I didn't notice that. I spotted a bar with swinging doors and cheerful music and talk spilling out, and pushed my way in. All conversation and even the piano stopped as a sea of faces – all black – turned to regard me, probably with more puzzlement than hostility but with plenty of hostility anyway. I remember thinking, "if I run they'll catch me". Fortunately, the bar itself ran along the wall next to the door and a bartender was nearby. I plucked up all of my courage and squeaked, "Can I get a beer?" It was all I could think of. He looked at me curiously and said "Where you from?" – "Australia," I said, and the talk and the piano resumed. A couple of blokes, ex-Marines, had been on R&R in Sydney during the Vietnam War and took me under their wing. They bought me drinks, introduced me to their friends and walked me back to the Y when I told them I had to ride the next day. "You ain't goin' by yourself," one of them laughed.

Everyone in Georgia speaks with that seductive southern drawl. It makes an enquiry as to one's preferred beverage in a diner sound like an invitation to view the bedroom... Yes, I liked Georgia even though my next breakfast was taken in a chain restaurant called a Huddle House and was awful. I promised myself I'd stick to the little private diners after that. They're almost always excellent value.

The fine for littering the roads in Georgia is a rather desultory $25, after a high in Connecticut and Florida of $500. It's still pretty clean, for all that, and the people are very friendly. A Mustang full of young ladies followed me for two or three miles while they figured out my number-plate and all the stickers on the back of the bike, then they went past tooting the horn, waving and throwing peace signs.

Another thunderstorm caught me down in Alabama and followed me almost to the campsite out on one of the sand islands, called Keys, off the coast. There were "Don't Feed the Alligators" signs up all over the site. Can you imagine an alligator coming up and stealing your picnic basket?

The men down here were all carefully haircut, and the women even more carefully made up. But I still found no hassles, in the bars or elsewhere – as long as I managed to keep the conversation off colour.

A seriously impressive sight down on the Gulf of Mexico.

Whites in the South are a long way from accepting blacks as equals, and are very careful to make a point of that in conversation with strangers. As a visitor, I found myself in a difficult position, and I'm afraid I compromised by keeping my mouth shut. I pondered all this one morning over that great American institution, the bottomless cup of coffee, in Hazel's Diner in Gulf Shores. No conclusion emerged, I'm sorry to say, beyond the obvious fact that I ought to stay out of something I knew far too little about. That, much as I regret it, was my contribution to civil rights in the South.

Mobile was resplendent with magnolia and old Southern mansions, and the long ride along the coast to New Orleans rather reminded me of Australia. The road could have been running along Port Philip Bay, or through Brighton-le-Sands in Sydney, going by the architecture and the flora.

New Orleans was rather different, of course. I teamed up with Matt, a Canadian who pulled in at the YMCA at almost the same time as I did. He was on a Honda CB900 Special, a bike rather better suited to US touring than poor old Hardly. Matt and I went out to do the town together. The Gumbo Shop came first – a restaurant specialising in the traditional Creole cooking – and was surprisingly cheap. Then we hit the hustle and bustle. First a walk up Bourbon Street, with its tourist glitter, and then a visit to Preservation Hall, one of the few places where genuine New Orleans Jazz is still played – well, genuine for the tourists. There's no booze available, so our next stop was Pat O'Brien's Bar, next door, where we each put away a Hurricane, a monstrous $5 cocktail which seems to consist mostly of rum.

At Sloppy Jim's, over a few glasses of draught Dixie Beer, we tried to collate our ideas of New Orleans. It's a strange town. The place is full of tourists, yet it doesn't feel like a tourist town. Everybody has a good time, except perhaps for the crowds in the assembly-line bars on Bourbon Street. Off the main drag, the people in the bars and restaurants are there to enjoy themselves – and they're not about to be cheated of it; as a couple we met in O'Brien's said: "We're from

Hanging around Bourbon Street with a Canadian biker I met on the road.

Jackson, Mississippi, but when we want to have a good time, we come down hyar!"

I did my laundry the next day in a laundromat supervised by one of the descendants of Marie Laveau, the famous witch. At least I presume that she was a descendant – she looked and acted like it, and she was certainly in the right business. It was hot again when I braved the spaghetti of roads leading out of town and eventually over Lake Pontchartrain on the 24-mile-long causeway.

CHAPTER 32

The North Again

"America the beautiful,
Let me sing of thee;
Burger King and Dairy Queen
From sea to shining sea."

ADA LOUISE HUXTABLE

The way north was all corpses of armadillos slaughtered by cars, and poorly surfaced but pretty little roads. Then I reached the Natchez Trace, another route like the Blue Ridge Parkway, and followed that north to Nashville in serenity. I did stop off to pay my respects at Elvis Presley's birthplace in Tupelo. The suburb is now called Elvis Presley Heights. I visited Opryland in Nashville, a kind of Country & Western Disneyland, and had a good time. The one thing that annoyed me was that I had to pay as much as a car driver to park. This is fairly common in the US – there are no parking or toll concessions for bikes.

A few days later I reached Ann Arbor, Michigan, and another friend of a friend. Victoria and her parents welcomed me with open arms and supplied a sort of replacement home for a few days. I really needed it by this time, too. It does get lonely out on the road, even if you speak the local language. One sight in Ann Arbor that I will always remember is the sign at the Farmers' Market that says "No pets, bicycles or solicitors".

The bike got a much-needed and fast service. Then it took me north again, up through the Norman Rockwell country that makes up central Michigan, to Sleeping Bear Dunes on Lake Michigan. In the campsite that night I had a steady stream of visitors, fascinated by the sight of the little bike. I scored a dinner invitation, a gift of a kilo of smoked fish (fishing is big up here) and an evening sitting around drinking other people's beer. Very nice.

Not so friendly was the gun shop I saw the next day, offering free targets – large pictures of the Ayatollah Khomeini. This was during the time when the Iranians were holding American hostages, so I guess it was understandable. I reached the Upper Peninsula of Michigan with a terrible hangover. I had been attempting to cure a cold with bourbon, successfully, but was paying for it. John from Boulder rode into the campsite that night on a BMW R60/5, which he'd come over to the east to buy. Bikes are much cheaper in the Eastern States than in California or in John's home state of Colorado.

He had a story about being mugged, too. Apparently a 5ft tall mugger had approached John, who measured 6ft 4in, near Times Square and threatened him. "He ran away pretty quick", said John, "when I pointed out the error of his ways. But you gotta give him credit..."

I received the inevitable American invitation to come and stay before we parted in the morning, and took off a little before John. He passed me not long afterwards – the BMW had longer legs than the little Honda.

Naturally I paid my respects at The King's birthplace.

Upper Wisconsin was strange, with eerie abandoned-looking farms, rusting cars and run-down petrol stations along the highway. Things got better as I went farther west, and by the time I reached Janesville (the sign outside town just said "Janesville – a friendly place") I felt as though I was in the prosperous Midwest you read about. Towns like New Ulm, Balaton and Florence remind you of the many nations that supplied the settlers here. Mind you, it's also pretty boring country. Flat as far as the eye can see...

That didn't change the next day, but it was pleasant just the same. First, in the diner in Lake Preston, there was a complete set of Australian banknotes in a frame over the bar. I asked the bloke next to me where they came from, and he thought about his answer for a while before saying: "Feller useta live here now lives there." They're a concise lot in the Midwest.

At my next petrol stop I was invited in for coffee and brownies and then, when I stopped to tighten the chain, the side stand broke and the bike fell on my head. Fun all day! I slept in the campground in the Badlands that night, among the grotesque landforms that give the place its name. Spooky, with spires of soft rock reaching for the full moon, not a blade of grass or a bush on them.

The Harley shop in Rapid City was very helpful, and even managed to locate someone who would weld my side stand back on for a few dollars.

CHAPTER 33

The West

The Black Hills were pretty, especially after the long run over the Great Plains, but they're rather spoilt by dozens of tacky tourist traps. These fill the side of the road leading to Mount Rushmore and consist of such things as The Life of Jesus Wax Museum. The famous faces on the mountain itself look rather funny for some reason. Most of the Black Hills is totally unspoilt, and I found myself a little free Forestry Service campsite, where I was joined by two other riders. One had a CX500, the other an immaculate Harley Sportster. We lit a fire, drank what booze we had between us and watched the satellites passing over in the crystal night air. An elderly couple travelling in a camper joined us, and brought an enormous shopping bag full of fresh popcorn. What a night!

> "The American West is just arriving at the threshold of its greatness and growth."
> **LYNDON BAINES JOHNSON**

There's a system of balance in nature. After you've had a good time for a while, you get a bad time. Mine started the next morning with a flat tyre, and continued when the bike wouldn't start. Too high up, perhaps. We were a mile high. Much pushing finally got us under way, after I'd filled the tube with latex foam from an aerosol can. The bike laboured all that day against a strong headwind across Wyoming, the original cowboy country. Rolling grassy hills as far as I could see, broken by mostly dry water courses with names like Dead Horse Creek and Mad Woman Creek. It was overcast and chilly. But the sun came out the next day, and as I rode up to the Powder River Pass and Tensleep Canyon I thought of John Muir, the founder of the Sierra Club, who had said: "There is something in the sight of the mountains that restores a man's spirit."

I could have done with a little extra restoration in Basin, just on the other side of the mountains. The rear tyre was flat again, and I began the mammoth task of repairing the old tube. Mammoth because I kept pinching it while putting it back in. I wasn't yet used to the new set of tyre levers I'd bought, and the tube was very old. By the time the rear tyre held air again, the tube had six new patches on it and I retreated to the local bar to try to drown my sorrows. At least I found convivial company and a couple of good games of pool, and had my first taste of decent Coors beer – a significant improvement on the usual American slops.

I also got a lot of sympathy for not being American, and specifically for not being from Wyoming. The entire clientele of the bar assured me that Wyoming was the best place in the whole world, even if Basin, with its population of 700, might be a bit "slow".

My road west from this little oasis kept heading for a window in the thick general overcast, a window filled with sunshine and pretty little clouds. But I couldn't catch it, and it finally disappeared when I reached Cody, a town devoted to the memory of Buffalo Bill Cody, or at least devoted to the amount of tourist money that memory could bring in.

Up in the mountains once again, I found a bloke lying on the ground next to the most decrepit bike I have ever seen – and I've seen some decrepit bikes in my day, some of them mine. This was a 250cc Honda of indeterminate vintage, with one muffler tied to the rack and most parts held on either by grease or wire. The owner of this apparition proudly claimed the road as his and bummed a few coke cans of petrol from me – this being the most convenient receptacle to drain the petrol into – and went cheerily on his way.

Shoshone Canyon provided some exciting riding the next day, and took me up to the gates of Yellowstone National Park, and the snow once more. It was disappointing to learn that all the bears had been moved up to the high country, but it appeared that they had been having trouble with the humans. There was no danger of my meeting any bears that night anyway; I checked into the Old Faithful Lodge. Snow had been forecast for the night, and my tent suddenly seemed awfully flimsy.

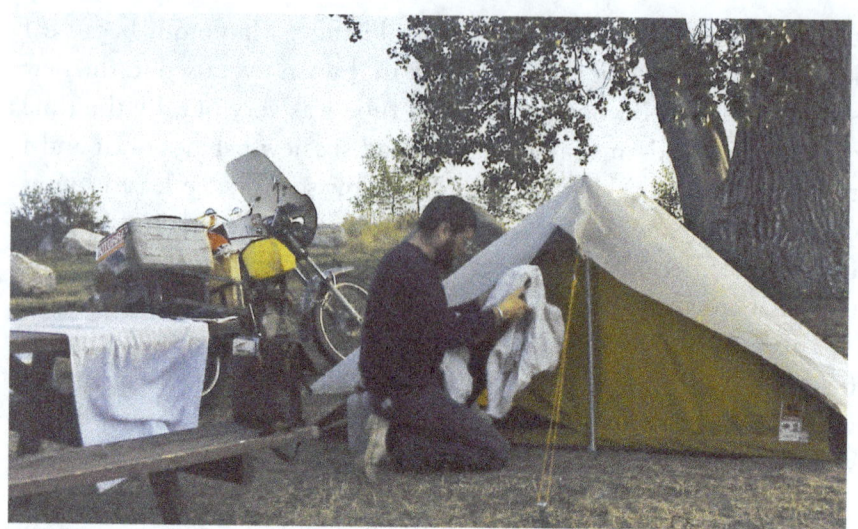
Camping continued to be an easy and convenient way to overnight.

Yellowstone Park itself was beautiful, like a piece of the world just after the creation, but I wasn't particularly impressed by the Old Faithful geyser. One Japanese bloke was, though. He spent most of the evening sitting at the bar's picture window, a barely tasted glass of whisky in front of him, concentrating on the geyser.

My evening was brilliant – I celebrated New Year's Eve with the staff. A trifle odd seeing that it was 31 August… It appears that a few years ago a party of visitors had been trapped by an early snowstorm towards the end of August. They reasoned that since they were stuck anyway, and it was white outside, they might as well celebrate Christmas. The staff have taken this up as a tradition, and there's always a Christmas and a New Year's Eve party towards the end of August.

I had a marvelous time meeting everybody, discussing politics, the MX system and the iniquity of the labour laws; all those things which are endlessly fascinating when you're drunk, getting more drunk and the surroundings feel good. One of the fascinating things I discovered that night was that if you're over 6ft 7in tall, you're safe from the draft. The US Army isn't set up to cope with people taller than that. So grow!

Not much of the US actually looks like this, but I did find some typical scenery.

When you're travelling on a tight budget, you repair your tubes rather than buying new ones.

All the celebrating must have disturbed my sense of direction (which assumes that I have one), because I took the wrong road in the morning. Instead of heading for Craters of the Moon National Park, I found myself on the road to Missoula. I made the best of it anyway and enjoyed the sweeping wheat fields and later the enormous trees of Lolo Pass. Just over the pass, an elderly chap on a KZ400 with a sidecar waved me over to the side of the road and offered me a cup of coffee. We stood in the thin drizzle, drank coffee out of his thermos and compared travelling styles. He was travelling even more slowly than I!

Outside Lewiston I had another flat tyre. This time I replaced the tube, but the bike needed new wheel bearings as well. The old ones had been severely knocked around from having the wheel removed so often. The bike was running much better now that I was out of the high country. Perhaps it would have been worthwhile to change the jetting after all.

I didn't need any directions to get to Portland – just follow the

Columbia River, right along the tops of the sheer cliffs that border its northern side. But once in Portland, I did need directions – just to find the post office. It seemed I had come to the wrong town. The first person I asked was a biker who had broken down on the freeway. He told me I wanted the exit two back. This on the freeway, where you can't turn around. After I'd found my way into town by myself, I asked a lady at a street corner. She did her valiant best, but became totally incoherent within a few seconds. We both finally gave up.

I then found the post office by myself, checked for mail, and made the mistake of asking for the road to the west. First my informant tried to talk me into going south. Then he told me to go down a certain street and turn left just before I could see the viaduct. What is the matter with Portland?

At Lincoln City, when I finally did reach the coast, I saw the Pacific for the first time since the beginning of the trip. In a way, my circumnavigation of the Earth was over.

But of course my ride was far from over, so I headed off down the coast the next morning. I stopped quite early at a lookout to take a photo of the fog swirling in to bathe the foot of the cliffs. When I got back on the bike, it was once again those ominous couple of inches lower. Another flat rear tyre – and this time there was an enormous sliver of glass in my nice new tube. Out with the tyre levers once again.

The coast was lovely, with forests and cliffs and dunes and hills and enormous trees – and a family of moose in a meadow by the river. The Youth Hostel in Bandon, a well-preserved old fishing town, provided shelter for three days while I relaxed, reading and checking over the bike. A new chain was overdue, so I made a shopping trip into the local metropolis, Coos Bay.

The Honda shop had a chain, and a small supermarket had some beer in white cans just marked "Beer". It was explained to me that this was what was known as a "generic" product – no brand name, no advertising, and therefore a low price. I bought a six pack. On the way back to Bandon I also picked an enormous plastic shopping bag full of blackberries. I was just congratulating myself on how well everything was going when the rear chain broke. Well, well. When will I learn not to congratulate myself? It was rather convenient that I was carrying the brand-new replacement in my tank box.

My new-found friend Larry thought that story was very funny when I told him in the bar that night. Larry was an extremely laid-back ex Marine, whose wife owned one of the three bars in town. He explained to me why he was happy with his life. "You know the story about the perfect wife being a deaf and dumb nymphomaniac who owns a bar? Well, look, my wife may not be deaf and dumb, but she owns this place, and as far as the rest is concerned..."

On down the coast, and past the gloomy but impressive hulk of Humbug Mountain, a block of stone between the road and the sea. I was in the redwood forests by now, which presented a problem in photography. Even with the widest lens I carried, I had to put the camera up quite a distance from the tree if I wanted to get both the top and bottom in, as well as myself standing at the base. So I'd put the camera on the tripod, set the self-timer and run like hell to get to the tree before the shutter went off. I succeeded most of the time. Maybe it was the majesty of the trees, but I started to do some rather serious thinking about what this trip had taught me, and how I had changed in the last two and a half years. I could come up with very little, except that I missed Annie badly. It's probably not so much that there's little to learn on this kind of trip . . . it's more that I'm incorrigible. After all, I'd coped pretty well with all the different cultures ... hadn't I?

I had looked forward to discussing all this with Ted Simon, who had written a marvelous book called *Jupiter's Travels* about his own circumnavigation of the globe. Ted now lived in San Francisco, and mutual acquaintances had given me his address and telephone number. But when I rang, it was to discover that he had just become a father – and swapping ideas about bike travel was the farthest thing from his mind. I could hardly blame him!

When I got out of the phone box, the bike refused to start again. The poor little 250 XL had been mistreated for so long that it was finally rebelling. Even pushing wouldn't do it. As it happened, the

This is a really bad photo, but I had to show the bike and a cable car together.

phone box was outside the Municipal Offices for the small town I was in, so I went in there looking for pushers. The Sheriff, Deputy Sheriff and the Fire Chief all lent a hand, and the bike - out of respect, I guess - fired straight away.

Through the coastal fog, I rode the last few miles into San Francisco. The fog was eerie, somehow - I had the constant feeling that there was an enormous eye, just above the fog, looking for me. California was beginning to affect me, I guess. They do say that the place has more religious nuts than any other place on Earth. Maybe it's catching. Once in the city, having crossed a Golden Gate Bridge whose upper beams were invisible in the same fog, I started looking for a bike shop to service the XL.

The Honda dealer's service manager was dubious. She indicated her crew of mechanics and said: "These prima donnas only like to put new bits on new bikes," something that the XL definitely wasn't. But she sent me down to Cycle Source, a small service shop run by the inimitable Jack Delmas. Jack is an ex-cop, and one of the friendliest, most helpful blokes I've ever met. His staff aren't far behind, either – Chris, on the spares counter, and Eddie, in the workshop, both helped me out. The shop was like a little home away from home. Eddie also got the bike running – and starting – beautifully. All at very reasonable rates. I celebrated by doing (more or less involuntary) wheelies up the steep streets of San Francisco, racing the cable cars.

SF is one of those rare cities that just feels good. Fishermen's Wharf is a tourist trap, but North Beach is full of great bars, with good music and imported beer. Although why they bother importing Bass is beyond me... Then it was time to turn east again, over the Bay Bridge and through Oakland and all the little valley towns to Yosemite National Park.

If Yellowstone is beautiful, Yosemite is exquisite. The soaring cliffs, yellow meadows and dark pine forests set each other off so well that the place hardly looks real. All development has been done carefully, and presents a low profile. The park is like a natural garden, from the delicacy of Bridal Veil Falls to the brute mass of Half Dome. Despite the lateness of the season, the campgrounds in the valley were full, so I camped in one of the free sites up in the hills. Smoky Jack campground was very pleasant in the half-dark, with campfires and

For some reason, I always take photos of this train when I'm in Death Valley.

stars both twinkling away. Despite the cold night, I slept well – no doubt partly due to the good offices of Mr James Beam.

Mono Lake was a little disappointing; its strange rock formations didn't really live up to the publicity. But I was thoroughly enchanted with an extremely attractive "flagperson" with one of the road repair gangs I met on the way south. Women are now a common sight in road gangs in America, but they seem mostly to do the less strenuous work. That's changing too, though. I saw a number of female tractor drivers.

At Lone Pine I turned onto the roller-coaster that passes for a road down to Death Valley. From 5000 feet it goes nearly to sea level, then back to 5000, down to two, back to nearly five, and then down to Furnace Creek, 178 feet below sea level. True to form, it was hot – over 37 degrees C – and it didn't cool down much at night. There were some German travelers camped next to me, and although I got some sleep on top of a picnic table in my underpants, they tossed and turned all night. Australian conditioning finally comes in handy!

I had a strong headwind the next day, and was nearly blown off Zabriskie Point lookout. But when I turned left at the ghost town of Death Valley Junction the wind was at my back and helped me along. The whole area is very impressive for its total desolation – over square mile after square mile not a blade of grass grows. It must have been a tough life working in the mines here.

Las Vegas spreads its rather unattractive tentacles far out into the desert. Housing developments go up on the flat, windy plain and some attempt is made to civilise it all by pouring great quantities of water into the ground to grow a bit of anemic lawn. I much prefer the desert itself. The town, however, is fun with its amazing architecture, combination loan offices/motels/wedding chapels/divorce offices, acres of neon and extremely single-minded people.

Something seemed odd to me about all the casinos, and it took a while before I'd worked out what it was. Unlike the equivalents in Europe, Las Vegas casinos were not styled like palaces or upper-class residences. Here, they were styled in Ultimate Suburban – their exteriors like a hamburger joint gone mad, their interiors like a suburban tract house owned by a suburban millionaire. Lots of flash, but no taste. Tremendous fun, all of it.

In the bizarre, broken-down little town of Chloride, I asked the elderly, toothless petrol-pump attendant where the campsite was. He pointed to the top of a distinctly bare hill off in the distance, and I decided to push on to Kingman instead. I followed one of the few remaining stretches of Route 66 in the morning, and rode through Coconino County, the home of Krazy Kat in the famous thirties comic strip of the same name. Meanwhile, dozens of grasshoppers hit my legs as I rode along – it was almost like riding through gravel as they rattled against my shins. There seemed to be quite a plague of them.

Still in beautiful sunshine, I rode up to the Grand Canyon.

The bike was still running well and lapping up the excellent roads of Arizona and Nevada. But it was getting a little hard to start again, so whenever I pulled up to take a look at the Canyon, I tried to find a slope to make clutch starting easier. Despite these concerns, I still found the Canyon stunning. The sheer size is overpowering, and it takes quite a while before the mind can take in its scale. It's very pretty, too, but it reminded me irresistibly of an enormous layer cake that's been attacked by monster mice.

From here, I turned north-east towards Durango and the Rockies. The old Indians at the roadside stalls where I stopped to buy turquoise souvenirs had the most awe-inspiring faces I think I've ever seen – except perhaps for some of the Tibetans in Nepal. Lined and sombre, their faces reminded me of photos of Sitting Bull. Did you know that he reportedly ate a handful of gunpowder every day to protect himself from gunshots?

The road past the bald head of Engineer Mountain and up to the 11,000-foot pass leading to Silverton was great. Quite aside from the fact that I was enjoying having corners again – despite its weight and nearly worn-out shock absorbers, the XL was fun on winding roads – I also got an altitude high. This happens to me occasionally when I get too high up, and I start making faces, singing, cracking jokes and laughing like crazy – all to myself. It also helped that I was back in the lovely Rockies, with forests of aspens and conifers on the steep slopes and that bracing, cold, clean air. Some of the aspens were already beginning to turn from green to gold. Winter was on its way.

I hurried to get to Denver, where I expected mail to be waiting for me, but of course the best-laid plans of mice and bears... Just outside Conifer, some 40 miles from Denver, my throttle actuating cable broke. I was on the very edge of the huge rampart of mountains that leads down to Denver, so I tried coasting. I got 18 miles before I ran out of hill! Then – at Bear Lake, to add insult to injury – I finally had to give in and switch the return cable with the broken one. This gave me a throttle control, but of course it now turned the opposite way – to accelerate, I had to turn the throttle away from me. Lots of fun in peak-hour Denver traffic!

By now it was too late to go to the post office, and when I got there in the morning there was no mail for me anyway. It's always a bit depressing when you're on the road for a while and don't get mail. You really feel lonely.

But I still had the address of John-with-the-BMW, whom I'd met in Michigan, so I went up to Boulder to stay with him. In traditional American style, I was made most welcome by all the inhabitants of his house and spent a cheerful few days there. Boulder is full of musicians and has an excellent library. I loafed and read and listened to music. My mail was waiting for me when I got to Denver again a week later, and my bliss was nearly complete. But I was still missing Annie, very much.

Down I rode to Colorado Springs along the row of frozen combers that make up the eastern edge of the Rocky Mountains, and then up and around Pike's Peak to Cripple Creek. An early mining settlement, this little town has now suffered the fate of all picturesque places in the US – it's become a tourist trap and derives its substance from the buses. It was still pretty, though, and the scenery on the way even more so. Some of the trees were now changing from gold to bright scarlet and the slopes were marbled with the different shades.

Sand Dunes National Memorial, an enormous dune formed by wind forced to drop its load of dust and sand by a mountain range, was not as impressive as the booklet had suggested, so I took my leave again and headed for New Mexico. Leaving Kit Carson's old fort to one side (he was the local hero here), I made Taos in the early afternoon. This has to be just about the ultimate in tourist towns – it gives the impression of having been built exclusively for the trade. Not that it isn't pretty, it just seems so phony. Perhaps I shouldn't talk. I only spent an hour there.

I slept up in the hills above Santa Fe that night, deep in another world. Everyone here speaks Spanish, the shop signs are in Spanish and the fluorescent Coors advertisements all say "*cerveza*" instead of "beer". I felt as though I'd made it to Mexico. In another sad case of prejudice, a white Anglo-Saxon-etc American I asked wouldn't tell me where any of the local bars were. He didn't think I really ought to drink with "those people".

From Santa Fe I took the back roads to Albuquerque and found myself back up in the mountains. It was drizzly and cold, too, but the road was well surfaced, narrow and twisty; I had a good time here. I also stopped in a weird little town called Madrid. It had obviously not long since been a ghost town, but now a great crew of hippies was busy restoring, shoring up and beautifying the wonky-looking timber houses.

On the way to Ruidoso and the Aspencade Motorcyclists Convention, I began to worry about the chain again. I'd had to tighten it rather frequently – neither of the chains I'd bought in the US lasted very well – and now the bike was jerking quite noticeably. I had all sorts of fantasies about bent countershafts (silly) and twisted sprockets (sillier).

Riding was becoming unpleasant. I made it to Ruidoso anyway, and spent a relaxed couple of days watching the bikes roll in. I'd been in touch with Honda, and they had expressed an interest in having my XL250 on their stand at the trade show, so, once the show started, I spent my evenings down there talking to the visitors – who found it

At Aspencade, I got to test ride a Harley-Davidson!

very difficult to believe that anyone could be crazy enough to ride a 250 around the world.

Days were spent drinking with my newly acquired friends Norman – who left his little dog Honda guarding their Gold Wing – and Bob, who'd ridden to the show on one of the very few two-strokes around.

Nothing much was going on, rather a disappointment after the bustle of European rallies, but it was great to talk to so many people, from so many walks of life, who were all devoted to motorcycling. I was a little surprised to see relatively few Harleys compared with the waves of Gold Wings that inundated the place.

I rode the new Harley Sturgis, and was very impressed with the belt drives, and spent a lot of time admiring the custom bikes. Unfortunately, they mostly looked as though they'd been put together out of three only slightly different mail-order catalogues. There was not really much variety. The trikes were spectacular, but once again there was little variety among them. On the third day, I won the "Longest Distance-Solo Male Rider" trophy, which still hangs proudly on the wall of my office.

Then it was off again – a straight run for the coast. Every trip has a limited lifespan, and after 11 weeks this one was gasping its last. So it was out onto the Interstate, a road I generally avoided, and off.

Seventeen miles from Yuma the steering went heavy. Inspection showed that the patch we had put on the front tube in the Khyber Pass had lifted. It was well over 35 degrees C, there was no shade, and in fact it was very similar to the conditions in which the tube had first given out. It went flat again just outside Yuma, so I had a new tube fitted. I rather begrudged that now, seeing we were so close to the end of the trip, but I couldn't be bothered with any more flats. In El Centro I also found an excellent bike shop, where they located a good second-hand Tsubaki chain to replace my old, worn-out one. So I was ready to face the last stretch with confidence!

The road to the coast was most enjoyable, through rugged hills on an excellent surface. In San Diego a solid wall of smog was waiting for me. I made my way down to the Pacific – nice to see an old friend again – and watched the huge oily rollers coming in all the way from Australia.

Up the coast into the rat's nest of freeways that is Los Angeles, and a stop at the Road Rider magazine office, where I was received very kindly and offered the use of a typewriter to belt out a few stories for them and refresh my traveling kitty.

I spent the last few days before my flight was due wandering around, by bike mostly, and sightseeing. I found Hollywood especially interesting – not so much the homes of the stars as Hollywood Boulevard. Then I had lunch with the friendly folk from Honda USA, entrusted my little bike to them for forwarding to Australia and climbed aboard the plane with the big red kangaroo on the tail.

I spent the flight planning the next trip…

AFTERWORD

The Bear, an overview

> *"If a little knowledge is dangerous, where is the man who has so much as to be out of danger?"*
>
> **TH HUXLEY**

Yes, I planned the next trip on that flight, and I have since taken it and many others. These days it's my job to take motorcycle trips, and to write about them – mainly for the publication I part-own, *Australian Motorcyclist Magazine*, for BikeReview.com.au and for ADVrider.com.

In the meantime, I have started four motorcycle magazines, edited another, and written for the likes of *The Bulletin*, *The Australian*, *Playboy*, *MOTORRAD* and *The Sun Herald* as well as numerous other (motorcycle) publications in Australia, the USA, Britain, Germany and New Zealand. I am proud of my contribution to the founding of the Ulysses Club which included designing its logo, and equally proud of the Bear Army, an organisation for some of my motorcyclist friends. "Busy, busy, busy" as Bokonon so memorably says.

Here's a short life history. I was born in post-war Germany and emigrated to Australia with my parents in 1959. I attended three high schools, the latter pair of which – Cabramatta and Bonnyrigg in Sydney's west – taught me a lot, some of it in the classroom. Sydney University welcomed me to study for a degree in Economics, which I dutifully pursued for two years until I woke up one morning staring into the abyss. I am still not quite sure what I was intended to be, but since that day I have known that it was not an economist. I departed from academe, having enjoyed being President of the Jazz Society and Chief of Staff of the student newspaper *Honi Soit*.

Taking a job as a graphic designer I worked my way up to art

All ready to take the bike down to Honda America – and then to fly home.

director of what was then the Australian Record Company. When I got tired of that I undertook the trip that is the subject of this book. On the way I met Annie, the woman who was to become my beloved wife.

    I have found happiness with her and my two daughters, Alix and Louise, to whom this book is dedicated. And I'm still out there, picking up bits of information to pass on to my readers; although I doubt very much that I'll ever get hold of enough to be out of danger.

bearfacebooks@gmail.com

www.ingramcontent.com/pod-product-compliance
Lightning Source LLC
Chambersburg PA
CBHW050310010526
44107CB00055B/2182